IV-V

Slavery and Servitude in the Colony of North Carolina

JOHNS HOPKINS UNIVERSITY STUDIES

IN

HISTORICAL AND POLITICAL SCIENCE

HERBERT B. ADAMS, Editor

History is past Politics and Politics are present History.—*Freeman*

FOURTEENTH SERIES

IV-V

SLAVERY AND SERVITUDE IN THE COLONY OF NORTH CAROLINA

BY JOHN SPENCER BASSETT, PH. D. (J. H. U.)

PROFESSOR OF HISTORY AND POLITICAL SCIENCE IN TRINITY COLLEGE, NORTH CAROLINA

Southern Historical Press, Inc.
Greenville, South Carolina

Please direct all correspondence and book orders to:
SOUTHERN HISTORICAL PRESS, Inc.
PO Box 1267
Greenville, SC   29602-1267

Originally printed: Baltimore, MD. 1896
Copyright by: The Johns Hopkins Press
ISBN #978-1-63914-129-6
Printed in the United States of America

AUTHORITIES USED.

Colonial Records of North Carolina; compiled by Col. W. L. Saunders, ten volumes, 1886-1890.

Laws of North Carolina. Revisions of 1715, 1752, 1765, and 1773.

Brickell. Natural History of North Carolina, 1737.

Hawks. History of North Carolina, 1858.

Weeks. Church and State in North Carolina, Johns Hopkins University Studies in Historical and Political Science, Eleventh Series, Nos. V. and VI.

Debates of the Convention of 1835.

Brackett. The Negro in Maryland, 1889.

Steiner. History of Slavery in Connecticut, Johns Hopkins University Studies in Historical and Political Science, Eleventh Series, Nos. IX. and X.

Ballagh. White Servitude in the Colony of Virginia, ibid., Thirteenth Series, Nos. VI. and VII.

Bassett. The Constitutional Beginnings of North Carolina, ibid., Twelfth Series, No. III.

—— Landholding in the Colony of North Carolina, The Law Quarterly Review (London), April, 1895.

Doyle. The English Colonies in America: Virginia, Maryland and the Carolinas.

Battle. Address on the Life and Services of Brigadier-General Jethro Sumner, 1891.

Biggs. A Concise History of the Kehukee Baptist Association, 1834.

Bernheim. German Settlements and Lutheran Churches of the Carolinas, 1872.

Fiske. The Discovery of America, 1892.

A Narrative of some of the Proceedings of the North Carolina Yearly Meeting on the Subject of Slavery within its Limits, 1848; published by the Committee for Sufferings.

PREFATORY NOTE.

The story of the negro in the colony of North Carolina must be reconstructed out of very unsatisfactory materials. If any point in this monograph should not appear to be treated fully enough it must be considered as due to that cause. Any suggestion of further facts on the subject will be duly appreciated.

I desire to acknowledge my indebtedness for assistance to Drs. Adams, Steiner, and Ballagh, of the historical department of the Johns Hopkins University, and to President L. L. Hobbs, of Guilford College, North Carolina.

J. S. B.

Durham, N. C., February 5, 1896.

CONTENTS.

SLAVERY AND SERVITUDE IN THE COLONY OF NORTH CAROLINA.

CHAPTER I.

THE INTRODUCTION OF SLAVERY.

The lives of the American slaves were without annals, and to a large extent without conscious purpose. To get the story of their existence there is no other way than to follow the tracks they have made in the history of another people. This will be a slow and, in a sense, an unsatisfactory labor. At best it can give but a partial picture of the real life of the slaves, yet it can give all there is to give. Those who in these days of a clearer view and a broader sympathy have come to look on the former bondsmen as a race having their proper place in the evolution of the human family, must be content to gather up as many facts as can be found and to regret that circumstances have made it impossible to obtain a more complete story.

To have come to America as a slave was not without an advantage to the negro, however disadvantageous it may be for his historian. The progress of a race is the lengthening of the experience of its earliest individuals. As each succeeding generation discovers new fields of knowledge, the experience of the former generation is thrust back to a stage in the individual's training previous to that which is considered the summit of an educated life. The facts which men now living are working out in laboratory and study will in a short time become a part of that general store of experience that will be standard knowledge for the schoolboy of the coming generation. That which any one learns from others is but the sum of the contributions made by those who have already lived. The experience which was the contribution of the earliest man must, therefore, be referred to a very early stage in the accumulation of this whole. Since his day the race has been but lengthening his life by successive steps in progress.

Now, the negro when he came to America was far back in this stage of progress. It is usually agreed that for ages he had developed none at all. When he came from Africa he came into contact with the most advanced type of experience in the history of man. It was his task to learn that experience. Viewing the matter from the standpoint of his development, it was his chief task to learn it. How could he best learn it? The answer is, he must learn it as another person who stands to this experience in the same relation with the negro, that is to say, as a child. The same reasoning which in all social systems recognizes the expediency of placing the child under the dominant direction of his more experienced parent, will be effective in showing that in the days of the earliest contact of the white man and the black man it was a useful thing for the latter that he took his first lessons in civilization in the rigorous school of slavery. Hard as the process was on the spirit of liberty in the black man, and costly as it proved itself in the life, the treasure, and the slow development of the white man, yet it is difficult to see how the aimless, good-natured, and improvident African could ever have been brought as a race to plow, to sow, to reap, to study, and at length to create thought, except for the tutelage of his slaveholding master.

The coming of the negro to the New World was due to economic causes. It arose from the meeting there of the two conditions of an abundant supply of undeveloped wealth and of a scanty supply of labor with which to develop it. This conjunction was due to a sudden widening of the spheres of industrial activities which in that day had been forced on the world. It was abnormal in itself and it led to an abnormal method of meeting it. It led to the forcible taking of men whose weakness made them unable to resist, and the bringing of them to work in the mines, forests, or fields on the American coasts. As these two unusual conditions of abundant land and a sparse population were in a measure relieved, the bondage that they had brought into the world ceased to grow, and then gradually grew less. That its final removal was accomplished by a most unhappy war against the smaller portion of this original slaveholding area was an unfortunate incident of the progress.

Conditions in the South were favorable to slavery. Large stretches of fertile land, warm climate, at once congenial to the negroes and enervating to the whites, and in some places unhealthy regions where white men did not care to work; all these helped to draw slavery to America. Planted at first in the Spanish possessions of the West Indies, it spread as soon as the mainland was settled along the entire coast from Jamestown, both northward and southward. The method by which this extension was accomplished is interesting. It may be divided for our purposes into two stages, an experimental stage and a stage of diffusion.

So far as the South was concerned, the experimental stage in the development of American slavery belongs to the history of Virginia, and possibly of Maryland. Chronologically speaking, that stage belongs to the seventeenth century. The Dutch traders, when they brought their human freight to Jamestown, were, according to the ways of trade, trying to open up a field for a new line of commerce. The planters that bought this new commodity did it no doubt without feeling sure that it would be a success. They found the Africans to be untamed, degraded, superstitious and dull. Could they make these into steady and reliable laborers? The partial success of the West Indies was before them, and they set out to try. In two respects they differed materially from the West Indian planters: 1. The harsh usage of the Spaniards in the latter region had destroyed the original Indian population, so that the whites were relieved of the ordinary fear of Indian atrocities. In Virginia it was not till toward the close of the seventeenth century that the savages were driven so far inland that the eastern part of the colony was safe from their attacks. Manifestly it would have been a dangerous affair for the colony to have attempted to absorb and to tame a large number of African slaves while there was fear of the Indians in their midst. 2. The nature of the task before the Virginians was different from that before the West Indians. The latter had gone into the business with the idea of establishing colonies of slaves, driven to the fields and back to the barracks as the Indians of the *encomienda* or as the slaves of the Roman *latifundium*. This was the Spanish ideal. The ideal of the Virginia planter, on the other hand, was that of the English country gentleman. He expected to live on his estate himself, and he wanted to group his slaves around him where he would know them, physic them, give them in marriage, and in his good-natured way train and swear at each one individually. To accomplish such an ideal demanded a great deal more in the way of absorption than was necessary in the Spanish system. It would take a much longer period of training to make the negro acceptable as a servant according to the Virginian's idea than according to the Cuban's. As a matter of fact, it usually took two or three generations to make him in any safe sense tractable. It was at least a half-century after the experiment began before Virginia was satisfied that its issue would be favorable. She then had the nucleus of a slave population which henceforth, both by natural increase and by further importation, she was rapidly to make an extensive part of her population.

There were three obstacles which everywhere in the South it was necessary to have removed before negro slavery could be widely diffused: 1. The Indians, as has already been said, must be either exterminated or driven into the interior, so that there should be no danger of Indian massacres. 2. The white population must become dense enough to be able to resist an attempt on the part of the negroes to strike for freedom. Tractable as the negro may have become in the course of three generations of slavery, there never was a time when he became so submissive that he could be considered beyond the probability of an insurrection. The whites understood this, and not until they had reached communities settled to a tolerable degree of density did they dare to introduce a large number of negroes. 3. The earliest importation of a class of laborers into the New World was that of indented white servants. Slavery had to encounter these in its period of diffusion in all the Southern colonies. There was a struggle between the two systems. This proved itself to be a case of the survival of the fittest. The negroes were fitter to be slaves than the whites and they remained masters of the field. When these three obstacles had been overcome the diffusion of slavery over new territory might go on prosperously.

When North Carolina was beginning to be settled, slavery was just finishing its experimental stage in Virginia. The people here were from the first satisfied with the profitableness of slaves, and took them with them as they went from the lower counties of Virginia to settle plantations on the shores of the Albemarle Sound. The three obstacles to diffusion they found it necessary to surmount. The danger of Indian attacks was not passed till 1712, when, having defeated and almost exterminated the Tuscaroras, they found themselves no longer in danger from such a source. It was about the same time that the people became densely enough settled to be able to handle the much dreaded negro rebellions should they come.[1] As for the indented servants, as will be shown later on, they never were a serious factor in the history of the colony. They came into it along with the earliest settlers, but the acceptance of slavery in Virginia had already sealed their fate. They never became numerous, and they

---

[1] It is of interest to note that negroes were not extensively introduced into Maryland till the beginning of the eighteenth century. (Cf. Brackett, " The Negro in Maryland," p. 38.) They were not introduced extensively into Virginia until near the end of the seventeenth century (cf. Ballagh, " White Servitude in Virginia," Johns Hopkins University Studies, Series XIII., p. 349, note).

were, from the conditions of life, never a very satisfactory kind of labor.

The manner of the spread of slavery after it had once entered the settlement is of interest. It reveals clearly the whole process by which the country yielded itself to the healthy ring of the civilizing axe. A lodgment was first effected in the extreme northwestern part of the colony, most of the people, free and slave, coming from Virginia. Either from natural increase, or from the capture of a few hostile Indians, or from importation from Virginia or New England, there was from the first an increasing supply of slaves. When a farmer moved into the colony he usually brought one or two slaves with him, or he bought about that number soon after he got himself settled. To settle a new plantation without negroes was considered a hopeless task.[1] Most of the men that came in to settle were men of small means, and they accordingly took up small farms. Having secured a piece of land, the incomer would go to work with his slaves to clear it, to plant it, and to build a house on it. He would not need much cleared land at first, for here the people did not devote themselves so extensively to the cultivation of tobacco as in Virginia. They had fine natural ranges for stock and raised many cattle and hogs for the markets to the north of them. If the farmer were thrifty he would have cleared his farm at the end of a few years, or at least as much of it as he did not want to save for his cattle range. At that time his stock of negroes would have increased. His most natural course now was to take up another tract of land, to divide his cattle and negroes, and, under the care of an overseer, to place a part on this new farm. This land cost him almost nothing, and if he did no more than support his slaves and cattle he would be getting wealthy from their natural increase. With two farms stocked, the increment of gain would be accelerated, and in a short time a third could be taken up. Then would come a fourth, a fifth, and in the course of a lifetime a

---

[1] Colonial Records of North Carolina, I., pp. 41, 601, 715, and VI., 745, 1026.

thrifty man might acquire a number of farms, each of which was stocked with negroes. This process was checked when the available land for settling in the older communities had been taken up, so that now if one wanted new land he must go some distance to the frontier. When such a stage had been reached the owner would begin to sell his slaves to those who were going to the new communities, or to allot them to some son or daughter who was going to the same place. Thus the negro went side by side with the white man in the van of the civilizing forces of the country.

The lords proprietors of Carolina recognized the value of slaves to the settlers from the first. In the Concessions of 1665, their earliest announcement of terms of settlement in Albemarle, they offered to give every master or mistress who should bring slaves into the province fifty acres of land for each slave above fourteen years of age so imported.[1] This custom, with slight variation, was kept up during the colonial period.[2] To make slavery secure in its legal aspect the proprietors declared in the famous Fundamental Constitutions that all masters should have absolute power over their negro slaves.[3] Thus the proprietors recognized the value of slaves in settling the lands. As long as the colony was in the hands of these owners, and also while it was in the hands of the king, slavery enjoyed all the immunity that was implied in these conditions.

Three distinct streams of immigrants entered North Carolina. 1. The immigrants from Virginia came earliest. These

---

[1] Col. Recs., I., 86.

[2] It is embodied in the instructions to Governor Burrington in 1730 (Col. Recs., III., 101-102); in those to Governor Dobbs in 1754 (ibid., V., 1133); and in those to Governor Tryon in 1765 (ibid., VII., 127). It is likely it was in that of Governor Martin in 1771, which unfortunately, it has been impossible to examine. It is well to note, however, that Gov. Johnston in 1735 said he knew of no such instruction. The leaders of the colonists declared that such had been the custom. It was decided not to follow the custom, but how long this was enforced does not appear (cf. ibid., IV., 60).

[3] Ibid., I., 204.

came in two rather well discerned movements. The former was that early movement of men of small means who came down into the unoccupied lands on the tributaries of the Albemarle Sound. They were not powerful and their settlements developed slowly. To them chiefly does the history of the colony in the seventeenth century belong. They brought a few slaves with them, though from the scarcity of records for this period we have very little idea of how many came or under what circumstances they lived. The latter of these two movements from Virginia came about the middle of the eighteenth century, or perhaps a little earlier, and filled up the counties in the northern and central part of the State. Edgecombe, Northampton, Halifax, Bute, and a part of Granville received the force of this movement. The people were largely the younger members of leading families in the northern colony, who took their slaves and moved south to build fortunes for themselves where land was cheaper. In some cases they were members of these same families whose extravagant living had made it necessary for them to gather up the fragments of property they still had left and to begin life again on the frontier.[1] These all brought slaves, and they used large numbers of them. 2. The southeastern part of the State was geographically distinct from the northeastern part. It remained for many years unsettled.[2] About 1730 Governor Burrington succeeded in turning immigrants in that direction. These people took up the rich lands around Brunswick and Wilmington, and gradually extended westward till they reached Bladen, Cumberland, and Anson counties. This stream brought slaves with it also. Having a good harbor, it attracted many people of means, not a few coming from South Carolina, and the rich lands along the lower Cape Fear soon came to be occupied by many rich and well-bred planters. This section had a

[1] See Dr. K. P. Battle's " Address on the Life and Services of General Jethro Sumner," p. 15.

[2] No account is here taken of the Yeamans colony, which soon removed, and which accordingly made no impression on the history of the province.

considerable trade with Europe, the West Indies, and the other colonies, and it is likely that it received most of its slaves through that trade. It became the most prosperous slaveholding section of the colony. 3. While this region was being occupied, the van of a third body was entering another part of the colony. Starting from Pennsylvania it came down the valleys of western Virginia and settled the central and western part of North Carolina. It was composed of Scotch-Irish, Germans, a few Welch, some New Englanders, some New Jerseymen, and not a few who from one or another place had already settled on the Virginia frontier. These were almost always small farmers, owning little property and very few slaves. Except for a few wealthy men who later came in from Virginia, or who came up as officers of the law from the older settlements in the east, they took small holdings of land and set out to clear and cultivate them with their own hands. As they progressed in wealth they yielded to the influence of environment, and slaves at the time of the Revolution were being used in considerable numbers among them. They were, however, never so strongly slaveholding as the east. It is well to remember that this section, especially the western part of it, remained till the Civil War the center of the anti-slavery sentiment of the State.

Estimate of Numbers.—To estimate the number of slaves in North Carolina at any time in the first seventy-five years of its existence is a very difficult matter. The colony was during this period increasing in population very slowly, and it was not till the end of the Tuscarora war, 1712, that the introduction of slaves may be considered as unimpeded. In 1709 Reverend John Adams, a missionary of the Church of England, wrote that there were in Pasquotank precinct 1332 souls, of whom 211 were negroes,[1] while in Currituck precinct there were 539 souls, 97 of whom were negroes.[2] Thus in

---

[1] Col. Recs., I., 720.
[2] Ibid., I., 722. There were at that time four settled precincts in the colony. Besides these, there was a new county, Pamlico, on the river of that name, which contained probably about as many people as one of the older precincts. These were the only white settlements in the colony.

each of these two precincts about one-sixth of the whole
population was black. It is likely that this proportion was
correct for all the precincts. Inasmuch as Chowan and
Perquimons precincts were older and in some respects more
thriving places, it is likely that they contained over 400
negroes. Pamlico, too, must have had some blacks; so that
it is a safe estimate to say that at this time there were about
800 negroes in the colony.[1] In 1717 Colonel Pollock, who
was one of the most intelligent men of the early period of the
colony's history, estimated the number of taxable persons in
the country at 2000.[2] Now, by a law of the Assembly of
1715 all negroes of twelve years or more, male or female,
and all male whites of sixteen years or more, were to be
taxed.[3] We know that in 1850 the ratio of negroes over
twelve years of age to the entire negro population was as ten
to eighteen, and that the ratio of whites over sixteen to
the entire white population was as ten to forty. So if we
suppose there to be still six times as many whites as blacks,
then we may estimate the number of whites in the province
at about 6000 and the blacks at about 1100.[4] In 1730 Governor Burrington wrote that the whites in the colony were
" full 30,000, and the negroes about 6000." [5] We have no
further estimate until 1754. In that year we have the first
census of the colony, so far as the records show. The clerks
of the several county courts, by instruction, made a return to
the Governor of all the taxables in their respective counties.

---

[1] Dr. Hawks says (" History of North Carolina," II., 340) that in
1700 there were 6000 whites in the colony. If we put the proportion of blacks to whites at one-sixth, this will give us about
1000 blacks in 1700, a number that would have been considerably
larger by 1709. Perhaps a better estimate would be midway between
the 800 and 1000.

[2] Col. Recs., II., p. xvii.

[3] Ibid., II., 889.

[4] In 1720 Boone and Barnwell, of South Carolina, put the total
number of taxables at 1600. They were probably mistaken. They
did not know the colony, and their language shows that they bore
it no goodwill. Pollock is a much safer authority (cf. Col. Recs.,
II., 396 and 419).

[5] Ibid., Vol. II., p. xvii.

The blacks were 9128 and the whites 15,733.[1] If we follow the ratios just estimated on the basis of the census of 1850 we shall have a total negro population of about 15,000, and a total white population of 62,000. Thus there was in the province an entire population of 77,000. Governor Dobbs pronounced the census of 1754 defective, the people, as he said he had learned, holding back their taxables.[2] The error could not have been very great, for when a year later he himself ordered a more correct return the total number of negro taxables was 9831, five counties being estimated in the manner just stated.[3] Another census was made in the same way in 1756, when it appeared that there were 10,800 negro taxables, five counties still being estimated,[4] and about 15,000 white taxables, giving totals of about 19,000 blacks and 60,000 whites.[5] In 1761 Governor Dobbs, writing to the home government on the condition of the colony, reported that there were not 12,000 negro taxables in its borders, and he added that the increase in the entire population came mostly from births, since but few people had come in since the French and Indian War.[6] In 1764 he placed the number at 10,000,[7] so that we must put his estimate at some point between these two numbers. This was a very erroneous estimate, however; for the very next year a census was taken by the method formerly used, and it appeared that there were in the colony 17,370 negro, and 28,542 white, tithables.[8] On this basis the entire population must have been about 30,000 blacks and 114,000 whites. Another census, made in 1766, gives 21,281 negro taxables,[9] eleven counties being estimated, and the figures of two more

---

[1] The returns for five counties do not distinguish between white and black taxables. In such cases the number of blacks has been estimated on the basis of the whites and blacks in all the other counties, which cannot be very far wrong (ibid., V., 320).

[2] Ibid., V., 461 and 471.   [3] Ibid., V., 575.   [4] Ibid., V., 603.

[5] These returns must be very unreliable. That of 1756 shows that in a majority of the counties the estimates had not been revised since 1755. This accounts for the great increase when we come to the returns for 1765.

[6] Ibid., VI., 613-614.   [7] Ibid., VI., 1027 and 1040.

[8] Ibid., VII., 145.   [9] Ibid., VII., 288-9.

being taken from the returns of 1765. This would give a total negro population of 37,000. A census taken in 1767 gives 22,600 black, and 29,000 white, taxables,[1] eight counties being estimated. This would be a total of about 39,000 blacks and 116,000 whites. These are the official returns, and constitute our only means of knowing with any degree of certainty how many negroes there were in the province. It ought to be stated that in 1772 Governor Martin wrote to the British Government that he had discovered that the former governors had overestimated the number of negroes and that the statement could be proved. He promised to correct the mistake,[2] but we have no evidence that he ever fulfilled the promise. He continued to believe in his theory, however; for in 1775, when he was a fugitive from the seat of his government, he wrote that there were very few negroes in North Carolina, except in two or three counties in the extreme southeastern part of the government, and that he did not think that there were over 10,000 in the whole country.[3] In the absence of any specific proof to sustain Governor Martin's position we must give the probability to the official reports, although the matter continues in more doubt than could be wished.

Unsatisfactory as these figures are, they indicate a tendency which is not wholly uninstructive. In 1709 about one-sixth of the population was black. In 1717 the ratio was about the same. In 1730 it was, according to Burrington, still the same. In 1754 there was a tendency for the ratio to rise, it being about ten to fifty-one. In 1765, when we come to a new census—those of 1755 and 1756 are of slight use—we find the ratio still rising, it being now ten to forty-eight. In 1767 it has risen till it is ten to thirty-nine. Thus we see that while the colony was growing slowly and was thinly settled, the ratio of blacks to whites remained comparatively constant, but that after the French and Indian War the negroes began rapidly to gain.

Importation.—The steadiness of this increase for so long a time indicates that it was due almost wholly to births.

---

[1] Col. Recs., VII., 539.   [2] Ibid., IX., 259.   [3] Ibid., X., 46.

Such rare information as we have on this point shows that the number imported was inconsiderable. When a person took advantage of the custom giving each newcomer fifty acres of land for each slave he brought with him, it was necessary for him to go into the county court and prove the fact of importation. The records of these courts, so far as we have them, show that very few persons proved their rights to land on this account. For example, in the court of Perquimons precinct in 1706, at which land was granted for importing sixty-nine persons, there are only four of these sixty-nine of whom we are sure that they were negroes, although there are six more whose names may be those of negroes; and all of these were imported by two men.[1] The king did all he could to facilitate the sale of slaves to the colonist by the Royal African Company. In 1730 Burrington was instructed to report on the condition of the company's trade in North Carolina.[2] That officer replied that up to that year this trade had been small, but that he thought that he could improve its condition.[3] It was probably with the same subject in mind that he reported three years later that the colonists had suffered greatly from not buying slaves directly from Africa. He added that under existing circumstances they had been " under necessity to buy the refuse, refractory and distempered negroes brought from other governments," whereas it would, he did not doubt, be an easy matter to sell a shipload of good negroes in almost any part of the province.[4] In a like spirit the king instructed Governor Dobbs, in 1754, not to allow the Assembly to pass any law which would prohibit the importation of slaves or felons,[5] as had been done in some colonies. The Assembly gave the Governor no occasion to enforce this instruction.[6] The con-

---

[1] Col. Recs., I., 649-656.   [2] Ibid., III., 115-116.   [3] Ibid., III., 154-155.
[4] Ibid., III., 430.   [5] Ibid., V., 1118.
[6] In Virginia, in 1708, Governor Jennings reported that in the past nine years the Royal African Company had imported into Virginia 679 negroes, while from other sources had come 5928. The reason for this state of affairs is not given (cf. N. C. Col. Recs., I., 693). About the same time Brickell wrote that the planters saved most of their coin " to buy negroes with in the islands and other places " (Nat. Hist. of N. C., p. 45; also p. 272).

dition, of importation may be seen from the fact that in 1754 only nineteen negroes were entered in the custom-house at Bath, and that the average number brought into Beaufort for the preceding seven years was seventeen.[1] In 1772 Governor Martin estimated that the total number imported into the province in eight months did not exceed 200.[2] These numbers refer undoubtedly to the number brought into the province through its custom-houses. The inefficient naval officers at the ports doubtless let a considerable number more than these come in without any duties paid, and there was always a number brought down by the land routes from Virginia. There is reason to believe that the latter route was the way by which most of the slaves came.

Distribution of Slaves.—Mention has already been made of the three movements of immigration which carried slaves into the colony. The eastern part of the country, speaking broadly, was strongly slaveholding. The western part was, for a time, almost free territory, and never had as many slaves as the east. This was due to conditions of settlement. Those persons who settled the west were used to tilling their own lands, expected to till them, and found it for a while more profitable to till them. Those in the east came mostly from eastern Virginia, where they had learned the value of slave labor and started with the idea that slaves they must have. This condition is well illustrated in a letter from Governor Dobbs in 1755. He is speaking of the people of the country and declares that above all they suffer from the lack of pious clergymen and good schools. This occasioned idleness, thriftlessness, and ignorance, " which, with the warmth of the climate and plenty they have of cattle and fruit without labour, prevents their Industry, by which Means the Price of Labour is very high, and the Artificers and Labourers being scarce in Comparison to the number of Planters, when they are employed they won't work half,

---

[1] Col. Recs., V., 144[h], 145, and 314. It is likely that an additional number were brought in without paying duty. The custom-houses were very loosely kept.

[2] Ibid., IX., 279.

scarce a third part of work in a Day of what they do in Europe, and their wages being from 2 Shillings to 3, 4, and 5 Shillings per diem this Currency, the Planters are not able to go on with Improvements in building or clearing their Lands, and unless they are very industrious to lay up as much as can purchase 2 or 3 Negroes, they are no ways able to cultivate their Lands as Your Lordships expect. . . . Young or new planters could not venture to take up Lands, and those who are rich can't get hands to assist them to cultivate, until they can buy Slaves and teach them some handicraft Trades."[1]   This condition of affairs he declared was still an obstacle to progress in 1764.   It was a natural outgrowth of slavery, and it was the price that the South always paid to her " peculiar institution."

The numerical contrast in the slave populations of the two sections is very great.   In 1767 there were in the sixteen counties which we may call eastern, that is to say those that were not settled by people who came the western route, 10,238 white, as against 12,307 black, taxables.   By the method of estimating which we have already used, this would be a total population of 41,000 whites and 21,500 blacks.   In the thirteen counties which we may call western there were by the same returns 19,448 white, and 9092 black, taxables. This would be a total population of about 77,000 whites and about 16,000 blacks.[2]   The greatest excess of slaves over white people was in Brunswick County, where there were 224 white, and 1085 black, taxables,[3] altogether about 900 whites to about 1800 blacks.   Reverend John McDowell, in speaking of the parish which made up this county, said, in 1762: " We have but few families in this parish, but of the best in the province, viz., His Excellency the Governor, His Honor the President, some of the honorable Council, Col. Dry, the Collector, and about 20 other good families, who have each of them great gangs of slaves.   We have in all

---

[1] Col. Recs., V., 315, and VI., 1026.
[2] Cf. Col. Recs., VII., 145, 288, 539 and 540.   [3] Ibid., VII., 539.

about 200 families."[1] Against this eastern country it is well
to place Rowan in the west. In 1754 it had only 54 black,
against 1116 white, taxables.[2] How many it had in 1767
does not appear, since its black and white taxables are not
distinguished in the returns.

---

[1] Col. Recs., VI., 729-730 and 985-986. Brunswick was erected
into a county in 1764.

[2] Ibid., V., 152.

CHAPTER II.

THE LEGAL STATUS OF SLAVERY.

The first law of North Carolina, if such it may be called, in regard to slavery was a clause in the Fundamental Constitutions. It ran: "Every freeman of Carolina shall have absolute power and authority over negro slaves of what opinion and religion soever."[1] This clause but expressed the legal concept of the time in regard to the rights of the American slave-owners. It was enforced not so much because it was a part of the Fundamental Constitutions, as because it fitted in with what was in the other colonies already good custom. It recognized the slave as a chattel. He could, according to the popular theory, be bought, bred, worked, neglected, marked, or treated in any other respect as a horse or a cow.

The earliest known law passed in North Carolina on the subject of slavery was included in the Revision of 1715.[2] This revision comprised as many of the old laws as were in force in 1715. The necessity of the case would have demanded a law fixing the status of slaves and servants at an early date, and it is probable that this law, or its chief features, was in force at a much earlier date than 1715. It was most likely in force earlier than 1699, since in that year we find a law which contained a provision in regard to harboring runaways[3] similar to one in the law of 1715.

---

[1] Col. Recs., I., 204.

[2] These laws are preserved in manuscript in the State Library, Raleigh, N. C., and the one in question may be found on pages 269-290 of that volume. It appears as chapter 46.

[3] Col. Recs., I., 514.

The Slave in Court.—By this law a slave could not be tried in the same court that was open to a freeman. If he had offended seriously he must be tried before any three justices of the peace and three additional freeholders who were also slaveholders, or the major part of them, and who lived in the precinct in which the offence was committed. The tribunal thus constituted was to have power to try the case according to its best judgment, to give sentence of life or member, or other corporal punishment, and to order the execution of the sentence by the regular officers of the law. It was to meet at such a time as should be appointed by that justice of the peace whose name' came first in the commission of the peace for the precinct.[1] The reason for this separate court, says Dr. Hawks, was that the slave might be tried at once, so that his master might not lose his labor while waiting for the time for the regular court to sit.[2] If a slave should be executed by order of the court, or if he should be killed while resisting arrest, it was the duty of this court to ascertain his value and to give a certificate of that valuation to the owner. This entitled the owner to a poll-tax on all the slaves in the government in order to reimburse him for his loss.

This act was in force until 1741, when a new " Act Concerning Servants and Slaves "[3] was passed. The provisions for the trial of a slave were thereby slightly altered. An offending slave was to be committed to jail by any justice of the peace as soon as there appeared good reasons for suspecting him. The sheriff was then to summon two justices and four freeholders who were slave-owners. These were to meet at the county court-house to hear all charges against the slaves. All the justices of the peace in the county who were slave-owners might sit on the bench if they were present at the trial, though not all could be summoned.

---

[1] In 1740 John Swann and John Davis were removed from their commissions of the peace in New Hanover County for refusing to act at the trial of a negro (Col. Recs., IV., 460).

[2] History of North Carolina, II., 205.

[3] Laws of 1741, ch. 24.

This court was given a broader jurisdiction than that possessed by the older tribunal. It was directed to "take for evidence the confession of the offender, the oath of one or more credible witnesses, or such testimony of negroes, mulattoes, or Indians, bond or free, with pregnant circumstances as to them shall seem convincing, without solemnity of jury; and the offender being then found guilty, to pass such judgment upon the offender, according to their discretion, as the nature of the offence may require; and on such judgment to award execution." The master of the slave, or his overseer, could appear at the trial in his behalf, but in defending him he was to see "that the defence do not relate to the formality in the proceeding of the trial" (sects. 48-52). This law remained on the statute book throughout the colonial period.

It was a part of the universal law of Southern slavery that a slave should not testify against a white person in the courts. In North Carolina this principle seems to have been recognized from the first; for Tobias Knight, when he was charged in 1719 with complicity with Teach, the pirate, urged in his defence that the prosecution had introduced the evidence of four negro slaves, "which by the laws and custom of all America ought not to be examined as evidence, neither is there [*sic*] evidence of any validity against any white person soever."[1] This seems to have been at that time a matter of the unwritten law of the colony, rather than a colonial enactment. At any rate, the first time we encounter such a provision in the North Carolina laws is in 1746.[2] It was then declared that "all negroes, mulattoes, bond and free, to the third generation, and Indian servants and slaves, shall be deemed to be taken as persons incapable in law to be witnesses in any case whatsoever, except against each other." This feature of the law of evidence was renewed from time to time till the Revolution,[3] and indeed it continued till the abolition of slavery.

---

[1] Cf. Col. Recs., II., 345.
[2] Laws of 1746 (3d session), ch. 2, sect. 50.
[3] See Laws of 1762, ch. 1; 1768, ch. 1; and 1773, ch. 1.

The denial of the privilege of testifying in court has been regarded as a great hardship to the negro. Inasmuch as it affected the more advanced of the slaves of the period just before the Civil War, this is a just contention; but it is well to remember that in the days when slavery was introduced into America there were two good reasons, as the whites thought, why the negroes should not give evidence against a white man. 1. They were in the lowest moral condition. Those who have not examined contemporary testimony on the subject will not easily imagine how the negroes lived. They were naturally ignorant, superstitious, and filled with intense hatred for those who made them slaves and held them as such. They were bestial, given to the worst venereal diseases and they had little or no regard for the marriage bond. Indeed, as Brickell says, marriage sat very lightly on them.[1] They were unchaste and mostly unreliable. 2. The Africans were pagans. Those few who professed conversion to Christianity could not have had any clearly defined idea of Christian principles. The mass who were unconverted could have very little regard for the Christian oath. How could such persons, argued the colonists, be allowed to imperil the lives of Christian whites? That such testimony should not be received was quite in keeping with the spirit of the times.

Not satisfied with denying them the right to testify against the whites, the Assembly, in the law of 1741 (sect. 50), enacted that if any negro, mulatto, or Indian, bond or free, be found to have testified falsely, he should without further trial be ordered by the court to have one ear nailed to the pillory and there to stand one hour, at the end of which time that ear should be cut off; then the other ear should be nailed to the pillory, and at the end of another hour be cut off as the former. Finally the luckless fellow received thirty-nine lashes on his bare back, well laid on. This, it must be confessed, was vigorous enough to reach the conscience even of a pagan. The chairman of the court before

---

[1] Brickell, Natural History of North Carolina, p. 274.

which the slave was tried was, however, instructed to warn the witnesses in the outset against giving false testimony, unless indeed such witnesses were Christians (sect. 51).

If a slave should lose his life while engaged in some affair of the colony's responsibility, the master would feel that he should not have to lose the value of this piece of property. He might also be disposed to impede the action of the law. To obviate this it was provided that any master who had lost a slave in dispersing a conspiracy, in taking up runaways, or in the execution of an order of court, should have a claim against the public, to be allowed by the Assembly. If, however, a third party should kill a man's slave, the owner would have no other recourse than an action for damage to property.[1] In 1758 the Assembly decided to try an experiment. They were dissatisfied with existing conditions. Paying for executed slaves they considered a hardship, and they thought that they had come upon a plan which would save the lives of the slaves and still act as a deterrent from further crimes. They enacted that except for rape or murder no male slave who had committed a crime which was ordinarily punished by death should suffer death for the first offence; but that on due conviction such an offender should be castrated, the sheriff to be allowed for the operation twenty shillings to be paid by the public. The court must fix the value of the slave before the execution of this sentence, so that if it should be the cause of his death there might be no dispute as to the value to be paid his master. Three pounds were allowed by the public for the curing of the slave's wounds. For the second offence death might be the penalty. At the same time it was ordered that no owner should recover more than sixty pounds for a slave executed or killed in outlawry.[2] This experiment to relieve the government of paying for executed negroes did not, it seems, prove successful. It was put into operation in at least one instance,

[1] Laws of 1741, ch. 21, sects. 54 and 55.
[2] Laws of 1758, ch. 7.

in 1762.[1] Why it was not continued we do not know. It would be charitable to suppose that the public mind revolted at its disgusting severity. At any rate, in 1764 a law was passed which repealed the provision in regard to castration, and raised to eighty pounds the limit at which slaves executed or killed in outlawry might be valued.[2] The next attempt in this line was a bill introduced in 1771, which provided that the several counties should tax themselves to pay for slaves executed within their borders. Such a measure would throw the expense on the slaveholding counties, and was evidently regarded as a relief by counties that had few slaves. It was introduced by Thomas Polk, of Mecklenberg County, where there were very few slaves. It passed the lower house, but was rejected on the second reading in the Council.[3] The same measure came up again in the Assembly of 1773, but it met the same fate.[4]

Runaways.—One of the commonest delinquencies on the part of the slaves was running away. Used to the forest life in Africa and accustomed to much severity on the farms of the frontier planters, it was no great hardship to them to live for months or years in camp in the swamps.[5] It seems, too, that there were not wanting at that time freemen who would help the runaways. The law against the practice was very severe. The act of 1715, which has already been cited more than once, provided that any person who should harbor a runaway slave more than one night should pay to the owner of the slave ten shillings for each twenty-four hours he had been kept in excess of the first night. He was also to pay to the owner any damage the latter might be adjudged to have received by reason that the former had harbored the runaway (sect. 6). No master, it was further enacted,

[1] Col.. Recs., VI., 742.   [2] Laws of 1764, ch. 8.
[3] Col. Recs., VIII., 355, 356, 403, 405 and 409.
[4] Ibid., IX., 404 and 418.
[5] The Dismal Swamp was a great place for these runaways. Elkanah Watson found them there in 1777, and they seem to have been there much earlier. See Watson's Journal, Wake Forest Student, December, 1895, p. 85.

should allow a slave to go off his plantation—except he be in livery, or waited on a master or mistress, or accompanied a white servant—unless he first gave the said slave a ticket stating the place from which, and the place to which, the slave was going. Five shillings was the penalty for violating this feature of the law (sect. 7). All persons were commanded to do all they could to arrest slaves off their master's plantations without the proper tickets, and in fact to arrest any suspected runaways or any slaves away from their homes with arms in their possession. A slave so arrested was to be taken before a neighboring magistrate, who might, at his discretion, order corporal punishment. He who arrested such a slave was to deliver him to the master, if he were known, otherwise to the provost marshal of the colony,[1] and receive pay for his trouble from either the one or the other at a rate specified by law (sect. 8).

A slave that thus came into the hands of the provost marshal must be kept safely. If necessary, he was confined and the public paid for his support; but if he was not unmanageable, the provost marshal might work him to pay for his keep. A slave thus in custody must be advertised by proclamation in every precinct in the colony at the next three courts after the date of arrest. The jails in the colony were at that time notoriously insecure, and provision was made that if the slave escaped from jail the provost marshal should not be held accountable unless it could be shown that the prison was secure, or that the marshal had connived at, or aided in, the escape. Any person who should kill a runaway slave " that hath lyen out two months," while trying to apprehend him, was not to be held accountable for it if he would swear that he did the killing in self-defence (sect. 8).

Any one who will examine the laws passed from time to time on any one feature of slavery will be able to

---

[1] The provost marshal was the high sheriff of the county. In each precinct there was a deputy marshal. When the precincts were changed into counties the latter officers were thenceforth called sheriffs.

understand with ease the whole progress of the public mind in the South in reference to the slaves. The whites started with the idea that the negroes must be kept from rebelling. They erected certain restraints on actions which looked like rebellion, or which might possibly lead to it. As time went on the negroes learned how to evade these restraints or to find new lines, which it was feared would lead to liberty. As these avenues were seen, new laws were passed which closed them to the unfortunate blacks. It was not the harshness of the dispositions of the whites, but the inevitable logic of their first attitude on the matter that made them draw cord after cord around the black man to make his bondage secure.[1]

In nothing is this process seen more clearly than in the law in reference to runaways. The slaves found means of evading the law of 1715 in regard to certain minor points. The law of 1741 re-enacted the law of 1715 and added provisions to cut off these avenues of evasion. It was enacted that the person who tempted a slave to run away should be fined, and the fine for harboring a runaway was increased. If the person so fined could not pay, or did not pay, the fine, he was to be sold by the court for such time as was necessary to get money enough to pay it (sect. 25). This provision referred undoubtedly to freemen, and the inference is that it aimed at the free negroes and poor whites, most of whom had once been bonded people themselves. That they should have tried to screen the fugitive negroes is not unlikely. Any one charged with attempting to steal a slave and to take him out of the province was to be bound over to court on the oath of one reputable witness, and if he was lawfully convicted he should pay the owner the sum of twenty-five pounds. If unable to pay this amount he was to restore the stolen slave and to serve the owner five years. If, however,

---

[1] Brickell, who wrote with an eye to attract immigrants, said that the planters continually put into force all laws against the slaves " to prevent all opportunity they might lay hold of to make themselves formidable " (Natural History of North Carolina, p. 276).

he had already sent the slave out of the colony he was to be considered guilty of felony, and might accordingly be condemned to lose his lands, and also his life (sect. 27). To insure that he who took up runaways should be paid for his services, it was ordered that if a slave were taken ten miles from his master's plantation the churchwardens should pay the cost of taking him up and then collect the amount from the owner (sect. 28). If a runaway could not speak English, or refused to give his master's name, the sheriff was to advertise him for two months at the court-house door, . and at each church in the county, or at any other convenient places (sect. 29). If at the end of a month the owner was still unknown, the sheriff[1] was to deliver the slave to the next constable, and he in turn to the next, and so the luckless captive was passed from constable to constable till he came at last to the central jail of the province (sect. 30). The cost of all this was to be paid by the owner if he ever appeared, otherwise the slave was to be hired out to some person approved by the county court or by two justices of the peace (sects. 31 and 32). To distinguish such a slave from others, as well as to mark him so that he would not care to run away, there was placed around his neck an iron collar on which were the letters P. G., meaning, presumably, "Public Gaol" (sect. 33).

Lest all this should delay punishment so long that the slave would not be properly impressed, the justice of the peace before whom he was first taken was to whip him as he thought best, not to exceed thirty-nine lashes (sect. 34). To get the slave to the central jail was not an easy matter; constables gave various excuses. To facilitate their journeying, the keepers of ferries were ordered to give immediate passage to constables thus engaged; and the church-wardens were directed to pay the ferriage and to collect the same as the other costs (sect. 37). Runaways that were

---

[1] At this time the older precincts had been changed into counties, and the provost marshal, with his deputies, had given place to a sheriff for each county.

thought to belong to another colony must be advertised in the Virginia and the South Carolina Gazettes (sect. 39). When slaves had gone away to the swamps, and were issuing thence to destroy hogs and other stock, there was nothing to be done with them but to make them outlaws. The law of 1741 did just that. It directed that in such cases two neighboring justices of the peace should issue a proclamation calling on such slaves to return to their masters. If they did not return at once, any person meeting them might lawfully kill them, " without accusation of any crime for the same "; and for the slaves so killed the masters should be repaid by the public (sects. 45 and 46). When runaways were taken it was the custom to put yokes around their necks, and these they were forced to wear until " they gave sufficient testimony of their good behaviour to the contrary." [1]

The Slave's Right to Hunt.—Severe restrictions were put on the slave in regard to his right to hunt. Hunting was the gentleman's pastime, and it may be that the idea that it was not becoming to allow slaves to engage in it had something to do with the passing of these laws. Still it cannot be doubted that the chief reason was the desire to keep arms out of the hands of the negroes. In this, as in so many other features of these laws, the whites were looking to the possibility of an insurrection. Carrying a gun also gave the slave an opportunity to kill hogs or other stock in the woods, and this it was desired to prevent.

The first law on this subject was made in 1729.[2] In that year the Assembly, while passing an act " For Preventing People from driving Horses, Cattle, or Hogs, to other Persons' Lands," and for other purposes, incorporated a clause which forbade a slave to hunt with dog, or gun, or any other weapon, on any land but his master's, except in company with a white man. The penalty for this offence was fixed at twenty shillings, to be paid by the master of the slave to the owner of the land on which the slave had been found hunt-

---

[1] Brickell, Natural History of North Carolina, p. 270.
[2] Laws of 1729, ch. 5, sect. 7.

ing. The manner in which this clause was introduced indicates that it was passed chiefly to protect the stock. The law of 1741 took up this subject also. It provided that any one who found an armed slave hunting or ranging in the woods without the written permission of his master should take him before the nearest constable, who, without further process, should give the said slave twenty lashes and then send him to his master. The master should pay the apprehender for his trouble (sect. 40). This clause, it was seen, might bear severely on the man who relied on game for an article of diet. It was accordingly added that this law should not prevent a man from keeping one slave on each of his plantations to take game for his family's use and to drive away such animals as were destroying stock. Any slave who was thus set apart as his master's hunter must carry with him a certificate signed by his master, and countersigned by the chairman of the county court, stating that he had the right to carry a gun. If he were caught without this certificate he was whipped (sects. 41 and 42).

These were, without question, harsh laws, and they stood for a severe spirit of repression on the part of the dominant Assemblymen. Their very severity seems to have partly defeated them. It is pleasant to know that the spirit of the law was here harsher than the practice of the people. This we know from the preamble of an act passed in 1753.[1] Among other things it declared that " the remedy in the said act [the law of 1741] provided has proved ineffectual to restrain many slaves in divers parts of this province from going armed, which may prove of dangerous consequences." The truth about the matter is most likely that the good nature of the whites revolted at the harshness of the law when they were called on to apply it in individual cases, and that as a result many negroes who were known to be trustworthy carried guns and were not apprehended. The Assembly, looking at the affair from the standpoint of theory, took no such view. They now passed a law in which the

---

[1] Laws of 1753, ch. 6.

master's responsibility was taken into account. It enacted that no slave should hunt in the woods with a gun unless his master would give bond for his good behavior; and that if any one should suffer an injury at the hands of such a slave he could recover the amount of the damage from the master's bondsmen (sect. 2). No slave should carry a gun on a plantation on which no crop was planted, and only one should carry a gun on a cultivated plantation; "and the master, mistress, or overseer of any slave with whom shall be found any gun, sword, or other weapon contrary to the true intent and meaning of this and the before-recited act, shall forfeit and pay to the person finding the same the sum of twenty shillings proclamation money, . . . any punishment inflicted on the slave, forfeiture of the gun, sword, or other weapon notwithstanding; unless such master, mistress, or overseer shall by oath or other proof make appear that such a slave carrying a gun, sword, or other weapon was without their consent or knowledge" (sect. 3). In this way a master was held to a stricter account, and through him the slaves were probably better kept in hand.

It was also thought that the slaves should be watched more closely by the civil authority. To that end the courts, if they saw fit, were directed to divide the counties into districts and to appoint three searchers in each district. Four times a year, or oftener, these should search as privately as possible the quarters and places of resort of the slaves to find guns or other weapons. Any arms thus found they were to seize and have for their own use (sects. 4 and 7). This, it seems, was the first appearance in the State of the patrole, an institution which the slave eventually learned to dread perhaps next to the bloodhounds. It was also provided that a slave with no certificate from his master could not hunt with a dog, and any one who caught him violating this clause might kill the dog and have the slave whipped by the nearest magistrate, not exceeding thirty lashes (sect. 8).

An abuse by both whites and blacks was hunting at night with guns. Those who were so disposed might by that means

easily kill a hog or a cow and claim that it was an accident.
To guard against this the Assembly in 1766 placed a fine
of five pounds on any person hunting for deer at night.[1] This
law was renewed in 1770,[2] and in 1773 it was amended so
as to include slaves. It was then declared that if any slave
were found hunting with a gun at night by firelight he
should be arrested by the person so finding him, forfeit his
gun to that person, and be carried to any justice of the peace
of the county, who, on conviction, should give him "fifty
lashes on his bare back, well laid on."[3] It was unlawful
for any person to kill deer from January 15 to July 15. A
law of 1738[4] declared that if within this time a slave should
kill a deer by his master's commands, the master must pay
a fine of five pounds. If he should "kill, destroy or buy"
any deer during this time without his master's commands he
should, on conviction before a justice of the peace, receive
on his "bare back thirty lashes, well laid on"; unless some
responsible person would become bound to pay five pounds
in lieu of the whipping.

The Slave's Right to Travel.—The keeping down of the
slaves involved a strict prohibition on any assembling or
communicating at night with one another. In 1729 the
matter was taken up by the lawmakers.[5] They then enacted
that negroes traveling at night, or found at night in the
kitchens of white people, should be thrashed, not to exceed
forty lashes; and that the negroes in whose company they
were found should each receive twenty lashes (sect. 8). No
slave should at any time "travel from his master's land by
himself to any other place, unless he should keep to the usual
and most accustomed road," on penalty of receiving not
more than forty lashes from him on whose land he might be
found. "If any loose, disorderly, or suspected persons be
found drinking, eating or keeping company with a slave in
the night time" they should be arrested and made to give

---

[1] Laws of 1766, ch. 18.   [2] Laws of 1770, ch. 10.
[3] Laws of 1773, ch. 18, sect. 3.   [4] Laws of 1738, ch. 10.
[5] Laws of 1729, ch. 5.

satisfactory account of themselves, or be whipped not more than forty lashes (sect. 7). This, however, was not to be construed to prevent a master from sending his negroes on business with a pass, or to obstruct the intermarrying of the slaves of neighboring plantations when they had received permission from their masters (sect. 9). This law remained in force until after the Revolution. So much did the white people fear that the negroes would plot insurrection if they could meet, that they forbade, as will be seen later on, the meeting of the slaves for religious purpose.

The Slave's Right to Property.—It probably occurred quite early to the owners of slaves to ask themselves what property a slave could own. If he were a chattel, a thing, how could he have a dominant relation over another thing? How the men of the seventeenth and eighteenth centuries in North Carolina answered this question we do not definitely know. We do know that at first they were lenient with their slaves on this subject. They allowed them to have cattle, and probably to cultivate small plots of ground for their own use. Later in this period they became more stringent and took away the right of holding cattle. The cause of this does not seem to have been any intention to carry to its logical sequence their idea of a slave's legal status. It arose rather from the thievishness of the negroes. Having stock of their own, it was easy for them to steal that of other people, to change the marks so as to make them conform with their own marks, and thus baffle punishment. This seems to have led to the several laws which gradually restrained the slave's right of owning property until it was finally extinguished altogether.

The first provision of this nature is found in the law of 1715. It restrained the slave's right to buy and sell, or even to borrow. It provided that whoever should sell or lend to a slave without the consent of the slave's master should forfeit treble the value of the amount of the trade or loan and be subject, in addition, to a fine of ten pounds, to be recovered by the master. That this was considered more a matter of public safety than an act of justice to the master is shown by a further provision. If the master did not sue within six months after he knew of the transaction, anybody else might bring suit and recover the fine (sect. 9). The law of 1741 modified this by reducing the fine from ten to six pounds, and by providing that if the offender could not pay the fine he should be sold by the county court for a term sufficient to pay it.[1] This feature of the law was further amended in 1773 by an act that forbade keepers of ordinaries to sell liquors to slaves against the will of their masters.[2]

In 1741 the Assembly took up the matter of the stealing of stock by slaves. Thievish by nature, the African in America became especially expert in petty larcenies. He was the more impelled to it because he felt that he had worked to raise the stock and ought to have a full share. At the time of which we are now speaking it was enacted[3] that if any negro, Indian, or mulatto slave should kill any horse, cattle, or hogs without the owner's consent, or should steal, misbrand or mismark any horse, cattle, or hogs, he should have his ears cut off and be publicly whipped, at the discretion of the court trying the offence. For the second offence he should suffer death (sect. 10). The law of the same year, which we have already quoted so often, was more severe still. It provided that no slave should on any pre-text raise hogs, horses, or cattle, and that all such stock as was found in the possession of slaves six months after the passage of this act was to be seized and sold by the churchwardens, one-half to go to the informer and the other half to go to the parish. This rigorous provision remained the law of the land from that time throughout the period which we have under consideration (sect. 44).

The slaves for their part seem to have been accustomed to allege that they stole because they were not properly fed. In some cases this was doubtless a true allegation. At least the Assembly seem to have thought as much; for in 1753

---

[1] Laws of 1741, ch. 24, sect. 14.
[2] Laws of 1773, ch. 8, sect. 9. [3] Laws of 1741, ch. 8.

they enacted that no man who had a slave killed in outlawry or executed by the order of a court could recover his value from the public unless he could make it appear that the said slave had been properly clothed, and for the preceding year had constantly received an allowance of one quart of corn a day (sect. 9). This was an insufficient ration, and an insufficient means of enforcing it was provided. To direct that the getting of it should depend on the liability of the slave to be executed or to become an outlaw was but a slight approach to justice. There ought at least to have been a plainly expressed injunction that this minimum ration should be given to each slave on pain of proper penalties. The same law further provided that if a slave who was not properly clothed and fed should be convicted of stealing from any man other than his master, the wronged man might recover damages from the owner of the thief. If we may believe Brickell, clothing of slaves was not an item of great expense to the masters. He says that children wore little or no clothing in the summer, and that many young men and young women worked in the fields naked but for cloths around their loins.[1]

The Slave's Right to Life.—The King seems to have been more inclined to compassion towards the slaves than the Lords Proprietors. The latter in their Fundamental Constitutions had given the settlers absolute control over their negro slaves. So far as we know, this remained their attitude toward slavery as long as they held the colony. Burrington, the first royal governor, however, was instructed to endeavor to get a law passed " for the restraining of any inhuman severity which by ill masters or their overseers may be used towards their Christian servants and their slaves, and that provision be made therein that the wilful killing of Indians and negroes may be punished with death, and that a fit penalty be imposed for the maiming of them."[2] The same instruction was given to Governor Dobbs in 1754.[3]

---

[1] Natural History of North Carolina, p. 276.
[2] Col. Recs., III., p. 106. [3] Ibid., V., 1122.

He duly recommended it to the Assembly,[1] and a bill to that end was introduced. It passed three readings in the lower house, but was rejected on the third reading in the Council.[2] In 1773 William Hooper presented a bill to prevent the malicious killing of slaves. It passed both houses, but was rejected by the Governor, because "it was inconsistent with His Majesty's instructions to pass it, as it does not reserve the fines imposed by it pursuant to their direction."[3] The matter was taken up again in the next Assembly, and an *Act to Prevent the Wilful and Malicious Killing of Slaves* was successfully passed. It was the last law but one that was signed by the royal governor of North Carolina.[4]

Two of the sections of this act are so full of meaning that it is well to give them in full. They are:

"I. Whereas some doubts have arisen with respect to the punishment proper to be inflicted upon such as have been guilty of wilfully and maliciously killing slaves:

"II. Be it therefore enacted by the Governor, Council and Assembly, and by the authority of the same, That from and after the first day of May next if any person shall be guilty of wilfully and maliciously killing a slave, so that if he had in the same manner killed a freeman he would by the laws of the realm be held and deemed guilty of murder, that then and in that case such an offender shall, upon due and legal conviction thereof in the Superior Court of the district where such offence shall happen or have been committed, suffer twelve months imprisonment; and upon a second conviction thereof shall be adjudged guilty of murder, and shall suffer death without benefit of clergy."

It was also provided that if the slave that should be killed in this manner be not the property of the offender, the slayer shall pay to the owner the value of the slave, to be assessed by the Inferior Court of the county; provided, however, that this act should not extend to those who killed outlaws, or to

---

[1] Col. Recs., V., 660.   [2] Ibid., V., 666 and 676.
[3] Ibid., IX., 398, 470, 663 and 664.
[4] Laws of 1774, ch. 31.

slaves who died under moderate correction, or to those who were killed while resisting their lawful masters. If this was all the relief that could now be granted to the slave, what must have been his rights in regard to his own life before this law was passed! It is impossible to fail to see that the last proviso, in that it gave a man the opportunity to allege that the killing had been done while the slave was resisting authority, or in process of moderate correction, went far toward annulling the whole law.

CHAPTER III.

THE RELIGIOUS AND SOCIAL LIFE OF THE SLAVES.

Religion.—There is no part of our subject on which we have more unsatisfactory records than on this. The earliest slaves in the colony, except in rare cases, were undoubtedly pagans. The people seem to have been content that they should have remained such. Indeed, if we may believe much contemporary evidence that has come down to us, the whites did not care very much if they themselves were pagans. In view of such circumstances it is not surprising that we are compelled to pass over as much of the seventeenth century as falls within our sphere of inquiry with but little comment on the slave's religious life.

Besides the indifference to religion on the part of the whites, there was another cause of the failure to convert the slaves. At first all the American colonists who had slaves had the notion that it was illegal to hold a Christian in bondage. The right to enslave a negro seems to have been based on the fact that he was a pagan. If such were the case, would not conversion enfranchise him? It was a matter of doubt in the minds of the planters, and since it was such they hesitated to allow their negroes to become converted.[1] It was in view of this feeling that the Lords Proprietors declared in the Fundamental Constitutions: " Since charity obliges us to wish well to the souls of all men, and religion ought to alter nothing in any man's civil estate or right, it shall be lawful for slaves as well as for others to enter them-

---

[1] Maryland in 1671 passed the law stating that conversion or baptism should not be taken to give freedom to slaves. In 1677 an English court gave an opinion that converted slaves were " infranchised." See Brackett, The Negro in Maryland, 28, 29.

selves and to be of what church or profession any of them shall think best, and thereof be as fully members as any freeman. But yet no slave shall hereby be exempted from that civil dominion his master hath over him, but be in all things in the same state and condition he was in before."[1] So important did they consider this feature that when they revised and abridged their constitutions in 1698 they kept it intact.[2] These Constitutions as a whole were never recognized as of binding force in North Carolina,[3] yet the people did not hesitate afterwards to claim its guarantees in points which were in their favor.[4] This guarantee might have been successfully used to protect the planters should a case have arisen over the point in question, and yet it left the matter with an element of risk in it that made the planters unwilling to allow the conversion of the negroes.

The condition that followed these circumstances is well seen from a statement of James Adams, a clergyman of the Established Church who was in the colony in 1709. He complained because the masters would " by no means permit [their slaves] to be baptized, having a false notion that a Christian slave is by law free." A few of the negroes, he said, were instructed in the principles of religion, but he says plainly that they were not baptized.[5] The missionaries of the Society for the Propagation of the Gospel in Foreign Parts preached vigorously against this notion. Giles Rainsford, one of these missionaries, writing from Chowan in 1712, tells how he had had much trouble to induce one Martin to allow three slaves to be baptized.[6] Four years

---

[1] Col. Recs., I., 204.

[2] Ibid., II., 857.

[3] See the author's " Constitutional Beginnings of North Carolina," Johns Hopkins University Studies, Series XII., pp. 137, 138.

[4] Col. Recs., III., 452.

[5] Col. Recs., I., 720.

[6] Ibid., I., 858. In 1715 this same man writes: " I have baptized upwards of forty negroes in this and the neighboring government in the compass of this past year "; but there is no means of knowing how many of these were in North Carolina and how many were in Virginia (ibid., II., 153).

later Mr. Taylor, another missionary, reported that he had baptized five slaves, belonging to Mr. Duckinfield. He had also been preparing several others for baptism, but the opponents of the baptism of slaves had talked so much to the owner about it that he had declared that no more should be baptized until the British Parliament should pass a law providing that slaves should not obtain their freedom by baptism.[1] This was in Perquimons.

It is by no means a compliment to the North Carolinians of that day that this condition was improved so slowly. The lack of any efficient system of schools and of any even tolerable supply of ministers[2] left the intellectual and moral status very unpromising. That little progress should have come out of these conditions is but natural. From 1715 until 1735 we get only occasional information in the letters of the few missionaries in the colony. From these we see the total number of persons that were baptized. The proportion that were slaves is very small, but from 1735 it begins to grow slowly. In that year Mr. Marsden reports that during his stay at Cape Fear he has baptized " about 1300 men, women and children, besides some negro slaves."[3] In 1742 another missionary writes that in New Hanover County, where there were 1000 whites and 2000 slaves, he had baptized 307 of the former and 9 of the latter.[4] From this time information is abundant. A continued comparison of the reports shows a steady increase in the baptized slaves.[5] The improvement in the social conditions that came with a denser settlement and a wealthier community made for the advantage of the slave. The reports of the colonial clergy now show proportions something like the following: In a parish where there were very many slaves, 124 white and 40

---

[1] Col. Recs., II., 332-333.

[2] Governor Everhard said in 1726 that there was not a clergyman in the province (ibid., III., 48); and in 1735 there were only three (ibid., IV., p. 7).

[3] Ibid., IV., 13-14.   [4] Ibid., IV., 605.

[5] Cf. ibid., IV., 793, 794, 795, 925, 1315; VI., 225, 233, 265, 315, 711, 729, 735.

black infants are reported as baptized in 1765;[1] in another parish it is 124 whites and 46 blacks;[2] in still another, 331 white and 51 black children are baptized in sixteen months.[3] The same man reports in 1771 that from the preceding seventeen months he had baptized 383 white and 65 black children.[4] Another clergyman, Mr. Taylor, writes a year later that during the past thirteen months he had baptized in his own parish 174 whites and 168 blacks; 93 of the latter and only 2 of the former were adults. He adds that the slaves " seem to be very desirous of instruction in their duty." This was in Northampton County. When he went into Edgecombe County on a preaching tour, there being no minister there at that time, he did not have such success. He baptized in three days 129 white and 4 black infants.[5] There was at this time no opposition on the part of the masters to the christianization of the blacks, and it is likely that the number of them in any one parish who were converted was due chiefly to the clergyman there. It does not appear that all the clergymen were so much interested in the slaves as Mr. Taylor. If we remember that in this period there were very few clergymen in the province,[6] and that there were many slaves in the parish whose masters were Dissenters, and consequently had nothing to do with a minister of the Established Church, we shall see that after all the number of slaves reached by these clergymen was relatively small.

The method of instructing slaves in religion was entirely according to the notion of the clergyman, so far as we know. In the earliest days of the colony the masters did not put themselves to the trouble to try to convert their slaves; yet in the later period they seem to have been more interested. Mr. Taylor, in speaking in 1716 about the Duckinfield slaves,

---

[1] Col. Recs., VII., 126. [2] Ibid., VII., 424. [3] Ibid., VII., 705.
[4] Ibid., VIII., 553. [5] Ibid., IX., 326.
[6] Governor Tryon was thought to have done a great thing when he raised the number of parishes that had ministers from five in 1765 to twelve in 1767; yet it ought to be remembered that there were thirty parishes in the colony, and that he had not after all provided half of them with clergymen (ibid., VII., 103, 457, 540).

intimates that all the efforts made to convert them were made by himself. His own method of proceeding with the negro converts he recounts as follows: "I hope I took a method with the negro young man and the mustee young woman, whom I baptized, which will please the Society, which was this: I made them get our church catechism perfectly without book, and then I took some pains with them to make them understand it, and especially the baptismal covenant, and to persuade them, faithfully and constantly, to perform the great things they were to promise at their baptism, and ever after to perform to God; and then I caused them to say the catechism one Lord's Day and the other another Lord's Day before a large congregation, which they did both distinctly and so perfectly that all that heard them admired their saying it so well, and with great satisfaction to myself I baptized these two persons."[1]   This method was assuredly as creditable to the missionary as to the converts, and it is evidence of a considerable degree of intelligence in the latter.

It was some time later before the public conscience was aroused to the duty of instructing the slave. In 1754 the instructions sent to Governor Dobbs directed him with the Council and Assembly to devise some sufficient means of converting the negroes to Christianity. This instruction was perhaps given to Governor Johnston, whose instructions we have not preserved, and it was renewed to Governor Tryon but nothing came of it. In 1760 Mr. Reed, the clergyman in Craven County, said that he would not baptize negro children unless their masters would become surety for their proper instruction in religion. The masters, he said, would not take the pains to do this.[2]   Mr. Cupples, in Bute County, wrote in 1768 that when he had baptized a number of slave children, the engagements for some were made by their masters and mistresses, and for others by older slaves who had already become Christians.[3]

Whether or not these converted slaves fared better than the unconverted ones does not appear. They were most likely in

---

[1] Col. Recs., II., 332.   [2] Ibid., VI., 265.   [3] Ibid., VII., 705.

the first instance slaves who waited around the dwellings of the whites, and who thus came under the religious influences of their masters or mistresses. As these were converted they would become missionaries to the field hands. Negroes were allowed to come into the dwellings of the whites in order to attend family worship,[1] and this must have had a softening influence on the relation between the two races.

Although the negroes were allowed to join any church they might fancy, they were not allowed to have a church organization among themselves. To have one was at once against the policy of the English Church and against the sentiments of the planters. At that time, as well as now, the negro knew but little distinction between church and secular organizations. The planters feared that negro churches might become centers of negro conspiracies. It was in this spirit that there was incorporated in *The Law Concerning Servants and Slaves*, revision of 1715, the following remarkable section: " Be it further enacted, That if any master, or owner of negroes, or slaves, or any other person or persons whatsoever in the government shall permit or suffer any negro or negroes to build on their or either of their lands or any part thereof any house under pretense of a meeting house upon account of worship or upon any pretense whatsoever, and shall not suppress and hinder them, he, she, or they so offending shall for every default forfeit and pay fifty pounds, one-half towards defraying the contingent charges of the government, the other to him or them that shall sue for the same." [2] This provision was aimed most likely at attempts to practice the negroes' old pagan rites as well as at the having of Christian worship. It seems to have become unnecessary, for it was left out of the law of 1741.

---

[1] Dr. Hawks makes this statement on the authority of a MS. letter of Rev. Mr. Taylor, dated in 1718. This letter it has been impossible to find (Hawks, History of North Carolina, II., p. 229).

[2] Laws of 1715, ch. 46, sect. 18.

So far we have dealt with the religious life of the negro only as it regarded the Established Church in the colony. It would be interesting to know, also, his relation to the various dissenting churches of the province. Unfortunately, we know but little about these churches during the colonial period. With the exception of the Quakers, none of them, so far as we know, opposed the ownership of slaves, and all of them seem to have received the negroes into full connection when they had professed conversion.

The first religious body to worship in North Carolina was the Quakers.[1] From the first their attitude toward the slave was humane and brotherly. As early as 1671 George Fox advised Friends in Barbadoes to train their negroes in the Christian religion, to use them gently, and after a certain time of service to set them free. In company with William Edmundson he visited that island, and so labored with the masters there in behalf of the slaves that it was falsely reported that he was stirring up the slaves to insurrection. Both of these men came to North Carolina, and it is likely that they left the same views there in the minds of their co-. religionists as they had taught in Barbadoes. The first time the subject of slavery came up in the North Carolina yearly meeting was in 1740, "when an epistle was received from the yearly meeting of Virginia concerning bearing arms, going to muster, and using negroes well." In 1758 the matter of "making provisions for negroes' meeting" was referred to a large committee; and it was agreed that meetings should be held at specified times for the benefit of the slaves at four designated places, and that a certain number of Friends should attend these meetings for the purpose of preserving good order. At the same time to the former queries which were regularly asked at the local monthly meetings, the answers of which were reported to the yearly meeting, there was added this query: " Are all that have negroes careful to use them well, and encourage them to come to meet-

---

[1] See Weeks, Church and State in North Carolina, Johns Hopkins University Studies, Vol. XI., pp. 230-231.

ing as much as they reasonably can?" In 1768 the subject next came up. The Western Quarterly meeting could not satisfy themselves as to the true intent of a clause in the discipline in regard to the buying of slaves, and on that they appealed to the yearly meeting. That body appointed a committee on the matter, which duly reported that the discipline ought to be understood "as a prohibition of buying negroes to trade upon, or of those that trade in them; and that as the having of negroes is a burthen to such as are in possession of them, it might be well for the meeting to advise all Friends to be careful not to buy or sell in any case that can be reasonably avoided." The Western Friends were not satisfied at this, and at the next yearly meeting asked for the absolute prohibition of negro slavery. The matter was not decided at that meeting, and it was only in 1770 that it was definitely disposed of. In that year the query as to slaves was made to read: "Are all the Friends careful to bear a faithful testimony against the iniquitous practice of importing negroes, or do they refuse to purchase of those who make a trade or merchandise of them? And do they use those whom they have by inheritance or otherwise well, endeavoring to discourage them from evil and to encourage them in that which is good?"

This was taking very advanced ground, but two years later the yearly meeting went further still and agreed that thenceforth no Friend should buy a slave "of any other person than a friend in unity," except to prevent the separation of man and wife, or of parent and child, or for some other good reason, to be approved by the monthly meeting, and furthermore, that no Friend should sell a slave to any one who was used to buying or selling slaves for gain. About the same time the Standing Committee formally declared its views on the slave trade in the most vigorous language. They said:

"Being fully convinced in our minds and judgments, beyond a doubt or scruple, of the great evil and abomination of the importation of negroes from Africa, by which iniquitous practice great numbers of our fellow-creatures with their posterity are doomed to perpetual and cruel bondage without any regard to their natural right to liberty and freedom, which they have not forfeited through any act of their own or consent thereto, but by mere force and cruelty—we are impressed with abhorrence and detestation against such a practice in a Christian community; for experience makes it fully manifest that instead of their embracing true religion and virtue in exchange for their natural liberty, they have become nurseries of pride and idleness to our youth—in such a manner that morality and true piety are much wounded where slave-keeping abounds, to the great grief of true Christian minds.

" And therefore we cannot but invite our fellow-subjects, and especially the Representatives of North Carolina (as much as lies at their door for the good of the people and prosperity of the Provinces), to join with their prudent brethren, the Burgesses of the colony of Virginia, in presenting an address to the throne of Great Britain, in order to be as eyes to the blind, and mouths to the dumb; and whether it succeed or not, we shall have the secret satisfaction in our own minds of having used our best endeavors to have so great a torrent of evil effectually stopped at the place where it unhappily had permission to begin.

THOMAS NICHOLSON,   JOHN SYMONS,
CALEB TRUEBLOOD,   JOHN SANDERS,
RALPH FLETCHER,   [and fifteen others]."

At the same time the committee wrote a letter to the London Friends expressing their approval of an address against the slave trade which the Virginia Assembly was about to present to the king, saying that they had spoken of the matter to some North Carolina Assemblymen, and that they hoped to get a like petition from that colony. They also referred to a law of the latter colony which restricted emancipation to cases of meritorious conduct, by which " such Friends as desire to liberate their slaves from principles of justice and Christianity are under a great difficulty." Thus while the king was giving instructions to his governors to allow no act to pass the Assembly to prohibit the slave trade, the Friends were forming their views to ask that it should be discontinued.

None of these declarations had gone so far as actual emancipation. It was but two years later, 1774, when that matter was destined to come up. Thomas Newby becoming dissatisfied with owning slaves, brought the matter before the yearly meeting. It was decided "That all Friends finding themselves under a burden and uneasiness on account of keeping slaves may set them at liberty by applying to the monthly meeting." Persons were also to be appointed to prepare instruments of writing suitable for emancipation, and to decide whether or not those whom it was proposed to free could support themselves. In the same year Thomas Nicholson was permitted to publish "Liberty and Property," a pamphlet regarding a change in the law of emancipation.

One step farther was taken before the limits of our subject were reached. In the yearly meeting of 1775 the Western Quarter again brought up the query respecting slaves. They desired such changes to be made "as would relieve some distressed minds." The committee to whom the matter was referred found that it could be settled only by the prohibition of buying or selling slaves without the consent of the monthly meetings, and, loth to act, returned the affair to the meeting as too weighty for them. The meeting then took it up and ordered: "That Friends in unity shall neither buy nor sell a negro without the consent of the monthly meeting to which they belong." The succeeding year the subject was again brought up, this time by the Eastern Quarter. After much deliberation, and a most earnest desire to settle the matter in the spirit of love, it was the "unanimous sense of the meeting that all the members thereof who hold slaves be earnestly and affectionately advised to clear their hands of them as soon as they possibly can; and in the meantime that no member be permitted to buy or to sell any slaves, or hire any from those who are not of our Society." Any one persistently violating this decision was to be "disowned as in other offences against the Church." Apart from its remarkable significance as being the culmination of several steps towards the abolition of slavery by the Friends, this action is most noteworthy for its display of the harmonizing power of the Quaker principles. For several years these people had had a disagreement over this question. It had been settled time after time only to be reopened. Step by step

the advocates of slavery had been pushed back.	Finally they
were defeated.	What did they then do?	They "were able
very affectionately to express their sentiments" and to make
the decision unanimous.	It was reserved for this little meet-
ing of simple Friends to show the world that the question of
slavery could be debated and decided without either side
surrendering itself to a passion.	In this respect it was
greater than the Congress of the United States.[1]

Thus did the Friends gradually come up to the position
of entire abolition, giving themselves up to the cause in 1776,
the year in which the great war for national freedom was
begun.	With the balance of the story we may not deal here.
It is sufficient to say that the Society had committed itself
to the cause of freedom, and that in so doing it had started
the first movement in that direction in the history of the
province.

The Baptists came into North Carolina at an early date.
By the middle of the eighteenth century they had become
strong in the central and eastern part of the upper tier of
counties.[2]	We know but little about them, however, for this
early period.	They seem to have received negroes into
church fellowship with readiness.	Mr. Barnett, a missionary
of the English Church, said that they allowed negroes to
speak at their meetings.[3]	Their kinder feeling for the slaves
is further shown by a reply of the Kehukee Baptist Association to a question asked in 1783 in regard to the duty of a
master toward his slave who refused to attend family
worship.	The answer was: "It is the duty of every master
of a family to give his slaves liberty to attend the worship
of God in his family, and likewise it is his duty to exhort

---

[1] For these facts on the relation of the Quakers to slavery the
author is indebted to "A Narrative of Some of the Proceedings of
the North Carolina Yearly Meeting on the Subject of Slavery within
its Limits, 1848." This is a rare pamphlet, only one copy of which
he has been able to hear of. That has been kindly furnished to him
by the Library of Guilford College, North Carolina. See pp. 1-12.

[2] Col. Recs., III., 48.

[3] Col. Recs., VII., 164.

them to it, and to endeavor to convince them of their duty; and then to leave them to their own choice."[1] Although this opinion was given in the aftermath of the Revolution, it no doubt voiced a spirit which had been in existence for some time previous.

There were many Presbyterians in the province, but unfortunately we have no evidence as to their relation to slavery. They probably did not materially differ from the members of the Established Church in that regard. Along with these ought to be put a considerable number of Lutherans and members of the Dutch Reformed Church.[2] The Methodists, whose introduction into the South was so closely connected with the religious life of the slaves, came so late into the State that they do not properly fall within the period with which we here have to deal.

Social Life.—Mr. Taylor, the missionary, writing in 1719, gave the North Carolina slaves an excellent reputation. He said of the Duckinfield slaves that they "were as sensible and civil and as much inclined to Christianity and things that are good as ever I knew any slaves, any slaves in this place, wherever I have been, and indeed so are the slaves generally in this province, and many of the slaves of this country, I am persuaded, would be converted, baptized, and saved, if their masters were not so wicked as they are, and did not oppose their conversion, baptism, and salvation, so much as they do." It is likely that Mr. Taylor's success in teaching the catechism to the two Duckinfield negroes had made him a little too hopeful of the race. It is also probable that the negroes he here came into contact with were superior to the average negro of the country.

Brickell, writing about 1731, probably came nearer the truth. From what he says we may divide the negroes in the colony into two classes: (1) Those who had recently been brought from Guinea, and (2) those who had been reared in

---

[1] Biggs, History of the Kehukee Baptist Association, pp. 59-60.
[2] Bernheim, The German Settlements and the Lutheran Churches of the Carolinas. Cf. pp. 148 and 235.

the colonies. The latter were much more manageable. This was because of training among Christians, "which," he said, "very much polishes and refines them from their barbarous and stubborn natures."[1] The former often rebelled. As soon as they rebelled they would take refuge in the swamps, whence they would issue to commit depredations on the property of the whites. Such fugitives usually made themselves very much dreaded on account of their cruel and treacherous dispositions. They had, however, one foe in the forests. The Indians, he said, had a natural and irreconcilable hatred for the negroes and delighted in torturing them. When they would meet runaways in the woods they would attack them vigorously, either killing them or driving them back to the whites.[2] The price of negroes ranged from fifteen to twenty-six pounds sterling, varying according to age, health and disposition.[3] The amount which the Assembly fixed as the maximum price to be paid for executed slaves was eighty pounds, proclamation money.[4]

The intermarriage of slaves was a matter of little ceremony. The masters of the contracting party must first consent to the union. That being arranged, the groom sought his bride, offered her some toy, as a brass ring, and if his gift were accepted, the marriage was considered as made. If the couple separated the present was always returned. This occurred often, at times against the will of the parties. If the women bore no children in two or three years, says Brickell, "the planters oblige them to take a second, third, fourth, fifth, or more husbands or bedfellows—a fruitful woman amongst them being very much valued by the planters and a numerous issue esteemed the greatest riches

---

[1] Brickell, Natural History of North Carolina, p. 272.

[2] Ibid., p. 273.

[3] In Virginia in 1708 the price was, according to Jennings, "20 to 30 pounds a head for those sold by the [African] Company, and from 30 to 35 pounds a head for the like kinds sold by separate traders, who in general have sold theirs at a higher rate than the Company." Col. Recs., I., 693.

[4] In 1774 we find a Congo negro offered for sale in Halifax for £140 colonial currency. Ibid., IX., 826-827.

in this country." The children belonged to the owner of the mother, and the planters took pains to bring them up properly. The slaves showed great jealousy among themselves on account of their wives or mistresses. With such money as they could pick up they bought bracelets, toys, and ribbons for the women.[1]

The marriage of a white person and a negro was from the first considered exceedingly undesirable. The law of 1715, already cited, provided that no white man or white woman should marry any negro, mulatto or Indian on penalty of fifty pounds, to be collected of that one of the contracting parties who should be white. It also stipulated that any clergyman or other person who should officiate at such a marriage should also be liable to a fine of fifty pounds, one-half to go to the informer and one-half to go to the public (sects. 15 and 16). Explicit as was this law, it did not succeed in preventing such unions. The records show that two persons were indicted within two years for performing such a marriage ceremony. In one case the suit was dropped;[2] in the other case the clergyman went before the Chief Justice and confessed, as it seems, of his own accord.[3] This was a year after the occurrence and no action was taken thereon at that term of the court. Wherever these unions occurred the whites who were parties to them were of the lower class. In 1727 a white woman was indicted in the General Court because she had left her husband and was cohabiting with a negro slave. The case was referred to the precinct court for trial. It came, probably, under the law against fornication and adultery.[4] So far as general

---

[1] Brickell, Natural History of North Carolina, pp. 272-275.

[2] Col. Recs., II., 591, 594, 602.

[3] In this case it seems that the clergyman confessed judgment in order to save himself from one-half of the fine. The Chief Justice reported the matter just as the court had finished its business. It is possible that the matter was taken up at the next term of court, the records of which are lost (cf. Col. Recs., II., 672; and Hawks, History of North Carolina, II., 126-7).

[4] Cf. Col. Recs., II., 704 and 711.

looseness was concerned, this law of 1715 had no force. Brickell, who was a physician, says that the white men of the colony suffered a great deal from a malignant kind of venereal disease which they took from the slaves.[1]

We have no evidence that any considerable number of the whites attempted to teach the slaves at that early date. If they did not try to impart a knowledge of religion to them it is not likely that they tried to teach them secular things. As the condition of the people became more settled, however, not a few of the household servants were taught to read and write. We have the slightest view of an organized effort in that direction. In 1763 Mr. Stewart, a missionary in the colony, writes home about a society called "Dr. Bray's Associates," which was conducting a school for the Indians and negroes. Mr. Stewart was superintendent of their schools in the province, but at that time the attendance was but eight Indians and two negro boys. He added that he hoped "that God will open the eyes of the whites everywhere, that they may no longer keep the ignorant in distress, but assist in the charitable designs of this pious society."[2] The tenor of his letter indicates that the society was at that time recently organized in the province. This is the only knowledge we have of it. What success it had we cannot say. The fact that it left no history indicates that it did little for the negroes.

Although the slaves owned by the very first settlers were few, those who succeeded them had larger numbers. Everywhere in the colonization of America the frontiersman has been a distinct species. Used to settling down on little farms on the outskirts of civilization, he has found it hard to become absorbed into the larger life of a settled community. It has most often been his fate to recover from nature a rim of forest land, and then giving that up to some wealthy

---

[1] Natural History of North Carolina, p. 48.
[2] Col. Recs., VI., 995-6. Brickell says that several slaves born in the colony could read and write. This was about 1731 (Natural History of North Carolina, p. 275).

habitant of civilized life, to move on toward the West. This happened in North Carolina. Many of the people who occupied their little holdings during the seventeenth century sold them early in the eighteenth and sought other lands for a song on the frontiers. The newcomers were men of means. They usually brought slaves with them.[1] Their coming marks the change from the system of a few slaves to that of many. The same process was facilitated in the newer parts of the country by the opening of the turpentine industry. Here slaves were very profitable, and large numbers of them were taken to the high tracts of long-straw pine which lay back from the low grounds along the river.[2]

The first experiences in the acquisition of the habits of civilization by the slaves had in them an element of the grotesque. Their masters were quick to see this, and in many ways did they become objects of amusement. Brickell speaks especially about their names. Among them he found Diana, Violet, Strawberry, Drunkard, Money, Piper, Fiddler, Jupiter, and Venus. These names suggest the habitual taste of the whites as much as the fancy of the negroes. The planters gave the slaves small patches on which they were allowed to raise tobacco for themselves. This they sold for money. The amount thus realized was supplemented by what they could earn on Sundays. Brickell says they used to gather snake-root on Sunday.[3]

Slave Insurrections.—The continued fear of rebellion made the whites very severe in dealing with recalcitrant negroes. Brickell bears witness to this fact. He says he had frequently seen them whipped until large pieces of skin were hanging down their backs, " yet I never observed one of

---

[1] Governor Burrington says that early in the eighteenth century a man from Virginia bought eleven adjacent plantations in the older part of the colony. The former owners moved on to the westward. On these plantations, on which white people had formerly lived, there now lived a white man, his wife, and about ten slaves. Col. Recs., III., 430.

[2] Ibid., III., 431.

[3] Natural History of North Carolina, pp. 274-276.

them shed a tear." He was once present when a negro was hanged by a verdict of the neighboring whites, because he had wounded his master.[1] The master had tried hard to save the slave's life, but the people were not to be moved. The slave-owners in the vicinity, according to their custom, brought all their slaves to witness the execution, hoping that it might be a wholesome object-lesson. Not all executions, however, were so mild as hanging. In 1773 a negro in Granville County was burned alive, his crime being the murder of a white man. In 1778 another was burned alive in Brunswick County for the same offense. Judge Walter Clark in speaking of this event remarks: " Doubtless there are other records of similar proceedings in other counties." [2]

The law against insurrections was as severe. Having begun to have slaves, there was the greatest necessity that the strictest means should be used to keep down any rebellion. In 1740 a law for this and other purposes was introduced into the Assembly. It was going successfully through that body when it was cut short by a prorogation arising out of a dispute on another subject.[3] This law was doubtless similar in import to the law of 1741,[4] which has already been cited. It contained a clause which provided that if three or more slaves conspired to rebel or to make insurrection, or plotted to murder any person whatsoever, they should be guilty of felony and punished with death (sect. 47). In 1755 the Assembly's committee on propositions and grievances recommended that " the searching and patrolling for negroes be made more frequent than heretofore," [5] but no action was taken on the recommendation. In the Assembly that met a few months later, but in the same year, a like recommenda-

---

[1] Brickell says this was the law. No such law is to be seen on the statute books. It is likely that this was a custom usually followed in these courts for negroes, and this may be what Brickell meant to say (cf. ibid., p. 272).

[2] See documents republished in the Wake Forest Student, Nov., 1895, and in the North Carolina University Magazine, May, 1894, p. 405.

[3] Col. Recs., IV., 542, 549, 550.   [4] Laws of 1741, ch. 24.

[5] Col. Recs., V., 299.

tion was made, but it met the same fate.[1]   While the province
was arming for the Revolution, negro risings were especially
dreaded.   The Whigs and the Tories were so nearly equal
in numbers that the slaves, if they should have united, would
have been very troublesome.   Moreover, it was reported,
and no doubt believed by many people, that the British intended to arm the slaves against the patriots.   This induced
the colonists to increase their patrole, and out of the excitement that was thus aroused came the only alarm due to a
reported insurrection of slaves that we meet in the colonial
period.

In Pitt, Beaufort, and the adjoining counties in 1775 the
report was spread that a certain ship-captain named Johnston,
of White Haven, who was then loading with naval stores in
Pamlico River, was inciting the negroes to rebellion.   From
the stories told by some negroes the whites thought they
had discovered " a deep-laid, horrid, tragick plan laid for destroying the inhabitants of this province, without regard to
person, age, or sex."   The alleged plan was to the effect that
through the teachings of Captain Johnston all the slaves in
that region had agreed to murder on a given night all the
whites of the houses where they (the slaves) lived, and then
to proceed from house to house toward the interior of the
province, murdering as they went.   Here, they were told,
they would find the inhabitants and the government ready
to aid them.   Johnston was just sailing at that time, and he
was reported to have said that he would return in the autumn
and take his choice of the plantations along the river.[2]   The
whites believed the story, and for a while the entire region
was in a fever of excitement.   The terrified people pursued
an imaginary band of 150 negroes " for several days, but
none were taken nor seen, though they had several times
been fired at."   This was as near a discovery of the real
movement as they ever came.   A number of slaves were

---

[1] Col. Recs., V., 548.
[2] Col. Recs., IX., 94-95.

arrested on suspicion, and some were whipped severely, but none were proved to be connected with any plot. The report seems to have been entirely unfounded. Indeed, it is not impossible that it may have been wholly concocted for political purposes. The charges that the British were encouraging the slaves to rebel, the British sea-captain, and the necessity of filling up the militia—all are factors which would have made the spreading of such a report not a bad piece of politics, as politics went in those days. At any rate the occurrence must have been advantageous to the patriots.

In connection with this idea one ought to mention the charges made to the same effect against the last royal governor of the province. The patriots charged that Martin, when he took refuge on a British man-of-war in the mouth of the Cape Fear, sent emissaries to arouse the negroes, and that the blacks were in fact fleeing thither. This charge Martin emphatically and indignantly denied. The only foundation there seems to have been to the report was the fact that the Governor's men had made some raids into the interior, in order to get supplies, and that on these expeditions they captured some slaves, which they took with them. The Governor wrote a letter in which he gave it as his opinion " that nothing could justify the design, falsely imputed to me, of giving encouragement to the negroes but the actual and declared rebellion of the King's subjects and the failure of all other means of maintaining the King's government." [1] This was taken as a threat. The patriots ordered the letter to be published. They said that after turning it " in every construction of language " they could only consider it " a justification of the design of encouraging the slaves to revolt when every other means should fail to preserve the King's government from open and declared rebellion, and a publick avowal of a crime of so horrid and truly black a complexion, could only originate in a soul lost to every sense of feeling and humanity and long hackneyed in the detestable and wicked purpose of subjugating the colonies to the most abject

---

[1] Col. Recs., X., 138.

slavery."[1] So far as this declaration referred to Martin's private character it was unjust; he was not a man "lost to feeling and humanity." His worst faults were, perhaps, obstinacy and lack of decision. His greatest misfortune was to have to stand in the breach in order to hold up an idea which the spirit of the people had outgrown.

---

[1] Col. Recs., X., 138a.

CHAPTER IV.

THE FREE NEGRO AND THE INDIAN SLAVE.

Emancipation.—Reference has already been made to the fact that as slavery in North Carolina became more extensive it became stricter. When there were but few slaves the white people believed that they could manage them with little difficulty. There was also at that time a tendency to leave the individual rather than the law to deal with them. As the institution grew—gaining, on the whole, on the whites in population, and perhaps as the slaves themselves began to show signs of intelligent organization, the dominant class began to draw tighter the cords of bondage. The masters viewed with suspicion any thing or any people who were disposed to stand in the way of the perpetuation of slavery. Now it was just this that the free negro would do. With no master to watch him, with a sympathy for the slaves, with liberty to go or come at pleasure, and with immunity from the prohibition of carrying arms, he was a very undesirable personage to the slaveholders. Looked at from the standpoint of the latter, limits must be put to the rights, and the making, of free negroes. As they realized this the more, the narrower did they draw these limits.

In the law of 1715 it was enacted that no one should make a contract for his freedom with a runaway or refractory slave, provided this should not be construed to prohibit a man from liberating his slaves for meritorious conduct. It was provided that in case a slave should be freed he should leave the colony in six months after emancipation, on penalty of being sold for five years to any one who would agree to take him out of the government (sect. 17). A way was soon found to avoid this by taking freed negroes out of the country for a while and then bringing them back. In 1723[1] a law was passed which provided that persons who should be freed and who should return to the country after leaving it should be sold into slavery for seven years. At the end of this term they must leave within six months or again be sold for seven years. Persons who concealed slaves thus sold, pretending that they did it for debt or otherwise, were to forfeit £100. The law of 1741[2] declared that no slave should be set free except for meritorious services, and that such services must be judged and certified by the county court. If a slave otherwise freed were found in the province at the end of six months, the churchwardens should arrest him and sell him at the next county court for the use of the parish; but if he should escape from the parish before the expiration of six months and should return thereafter, he should be sold by the churchwardens as just stated. This was a hardship, inasmuch as it restricted the liberation of slaves to meritorious conduct, to be judged by the court. It afforded a full opportunity, it is true, for the action of the philanthropic feelings of the county courts, but at the same time it gave that tribunal a chance to prohibit emancipation entirely, if it so desired. That it did not act favorably to the slaves is certain; for we find the Quakers in their letter to the London Friends, which has already been cited, complaining that this requirement hindered them in their purpose of emancipation.

Free Negroes.—The law of 1741, although it made emancipation more difficult, was yet more favorable to the free negro, since it did not require those who had been liberated by regular means to leave the colony. Earlier than this a great many free negroes had come into the colony. The Assembly, which had the power to condition a man's liberation on his leaving the colony, did not have the power to exclude from the province any free English citizen who in the beginnings of the government had been given the privilege of going into the colony and living there. This policy

---

[1] Law of 1723, ch. 5.　　[2] Laws, 1741, ch. 24, sect. 56.

was adopted also in the other colonies.[1]   It is doubtful if it kept the number of free negroes in any colony at a lower figure.   It simply meant that the free negroes of one province were driven into the next.   Had they been left in the regions in which they were liberated, where they could have been still under the influence of the old surroundings, they could have been managed more easily.   These were two of the sources of the free colored population.   Another was the children of white women by negro men.   There is evidence that not a few of such people were in the government.[2] Taken all together, there were a considerable number of free negroes among the people by the close of the colonial period.

The privileges of the free negroes were few.   They were not allowed to vote.   The election law of 1715 provided that no negro, Indian, or mulatto should have the right to vote for a member of the Assembly.   This being the only elective civil office in the colony, they were completely disfranchised.[3] This law was repealed by order of the King in 1737,[4] one of the complaints being that freemen as well as freeholders were allowed to vote.[5]   No further law was made on the subject till 1760.   In the meantime the basis of suffrage was fixed in the instructions to the governors.   It was thus arranged that no one but a freeholder could vote for an Assemblyman.[6]   The law of 1760 continued this arrangement, and went on to define a freeholder as a person who held in fee simple or for life an estate of fifty acres of land.[7]   This requirement gave little opportunity to the free negro.   We have no means of knowing whether or not any free negroes voted under it.   In 1835 when the constitution was revised there was a proposition before the convention to make them eligible to vote

---

[1] Hening, Statutes at Large, III., 87, IV., 133.
[2] Debates of the Convention of 1835, p. 351.
[3] Col. Recs., II., 214-215.   [4] Ibid., IV., 251.   [5] Ibid., III., 180-181.
[6] See the instructions to Governor Dobbs, ibid., V., 1110.
[7] Laws of 1760 (4th session), ch. 1, sects. 3 and 4.

when they owned \$250 worth of property. There were a number that would have been benefited by that provision at that time.[1] Possibly there were a few who would have come within a like provision in the days before the Revolution. Like the slaves, they had not the right of giving evidence against white men. The right of sitting on the jury they probably did not have. The law provided that freeholders "knowing and substantial" should be jurymen.[2] This was ample opportunity to exclude them, and it was very likely used. Although no evidence appears on the point, still it is extremely unlikely that one of them ever held office.

If their rights from the State were abridged, their duties toward it were not impaired. They were required to bear their share in the burden of government, on an equal footing with white men. A law of 1715 enacted that all slaves, male and female, from the age of twelve, and all "males not being slaves" from the age of sixteen, should be deemed taxables.[3] Free negro women were thus untaxed. They did not remain in this condition long, however. In 1723 a law was passed which provided that inasmuch as many free negroes, mulattoes, and other persons of mixed blood[4] had moved into the province, henceforth all free negroes, mulattoes, and persons of mixed blood to the third generation, male or female, of twenty years of age or more, should pay the same levies as other taxables.[5] Complaint was made of these immigrants "that several of them have intermarried with the white inhabitants of this province; in contempt of the acts and laws in those cases made and provided"; and it was ordered that all white persons so married

---

[1] Debates of the Convention, p. 60.
[2] Laws of 1746 (1st session), ch. 8.
[3] Col. Recs., II., 889.
[4] The term "negro" was not then so commonly in use as in more recent days. Until well into the second quarter of the nineteenth century it was the usual thing in North Carolina to speak of a free negro as a "free person of color."
[5] Laws of 1723, ch. 5.

be subject to the same tax as was imposed on the negroes. This, it will be seen, would apply more especially to white women married to negro men, since negro women married to white men, unless they were younger than sixteen years, would come under the former provision of the law. How many there were of this class we have no means of knowing. The law of 1760 to regulate the collection of taxes re-enacted the provisions of these two laws, except that persons of mixed blood were to be taxed to the fourth instead of to the third generation. This law continued in force till the end of the colonial period.[1] This bore hardly on free negroes. In 1755 a petition came to the Assembly from the counties of Granville, Northampton, and Edgecombe, praying for relief. The lower house of the Assembly "resolved that the matters in the said petition contained are reasonable, and that the committee appointed to revise the laws receive a clause or clauses to be inserted in the said laws for their relief."[2] It was ten years before the next revision of the laws, and by that time the matter seems to have been reconsidered by the Assembly. Three more petitions to the same effect and from the same region were presented before the Revolution, but without apparent results.[3]

Not only must the free negro help support, but he must also help defend, the government. The instructions to the royal governors ordered a census of freemen and servants, so as to ascertain how many could bear arms.[4] In accordance with the spirit of these instructions the militia laws directed that "all freemen and servants within this province between the age of sixteen and sixty shall compose the militia thereof."[5] By these laws an overseer who had the

---

[1] Laws of 1760 (4th session), ch. 2, sect. 2.
[2] Col. Recs., V., 295.
[3] Ibid., VI., 902, 982; VII., 614, 624, 653, 901, 946, 954; IX., 97, 146.
[4] Ibid., V., 1138. Governor Dobbs was told to make a census of the people, "free and unfree," with a view of deciding how many of them are fit to bear arms in the militia of the province.
[5] Laws of 1746 (2d session), ch. 1; Laws of 1760 (3d session), ch. 2; Laws of 1764, ch. 1; Laws of 1768 (2d session), ch. 3.

care of six taxable slaves was to be exempt from musters, and by the last two of these laws he should be liable to a fine of forty shillings if he should appear at a muster. Also free negroes between the ages of sixteen and sixty were required to work on the public road, as were also slaves of the same ages.[1]

If a negro claiming to be free should sue for his freedom, the case was tried in the white man's court.[2] The procedure in a case of this nature which has come down to us was as follows: A negro presented a petition stating that he had shipped from St. Thomas with a certain sea-captain who said he was bound to Europe, but who had brought him into North Carolina. Here the negro deserted and took refuge with Edmond Porter. He then asked that he might be declared free of Porter, who now claimed him as a slave. This petition was presented to the Chief Justice, who ordered the Provost Marshal to take the body of the petitioner and produce it at the next term of the General Court. Porter was furnished with a copy of the petition and served with a writ of *scire facias* to appear at the said court and show why the petitioner should not be adjudged free. In the meantime the Provost Marshal was ordered to hire the petitioner to some one who would give bond to return him to the next court. When the court met, evidence was introduced, arguments were made, and without reference to a jury the verdict was rendered by the Court itself. As the records have it: "The arguments on both sides being by the Court fully heard and understood, it is considered & ordered that the said petition be dismist."

The law of 1741, which has already been so often cited, had a provision on a subject of a similar nature. Any person who should import or sell as a slave any free person from any Christian country, or a Turk or a Moor[3] in amity with England, should on conviction pay to the person from whom

---

[1] Laws of 1764 (1st session), ch. 3, sect. 9.
[2] Col. Recs., II., 702, 703.
[3] Notice that Africans are not included.

the slave should recover his liberty double the price paid for the said free person; and the importer or seller must give bond of £500 to carry the said free person back to the country from which he was brought. Suit could be brought here on complaint to a justice of the peace, who was directed to call the alleged offender before him and to bind him over to the next court. There the case must be determined without formal process of law.[1] This was as fair to the plaintiff as, all things considered, it could have been made; but it must be remembered that the negro who brought a petition under this act labored under the disadvantage of not being able to give evidence against a white man. In many cases the negro's chief witnesses must have been negroes. This law was intended to cover also cases of the illegal enslavement of persons not negroes.

Indian Slavery.—The first slaves in America were Indians. The unsuspecting natives of the West Indies were seized almost from the first by the Spaniards and made to work the mines.[2] Although Las Casas succeeded in substituting the more vigorous negroes for the Indians, he did not render the enslavement of the latter entirely impossible. The Indians taken prisoners in war continued to be held as slaves throughout the English colonies on the mainland. This was in keeping with a recognized custom of the Indians themselves. In a few cases, too, the whites who landed along unsettled coasts could not resist the temptation to entice the natives on their ship and sail away to sell them in the settled colonies elsewhere. The first intimation we have of Indian slavery in North Carolina is of the latter sort. Lawson, writing of the New England people who had attempted in 1660 to plant a colony at the mouth of the Cape Fear, says they were driven off by the Indians, some of whose children they had sent to the North under pretext of educating them. The Indians became suspicious that the children had been

---

[1] Laws of 1741, ch. 24, sects. 23 and 24.
[2] For an excellent brief description of this phase of American slavery, see Fiske, The Discovery of America, II., pp. 427 *et seq.*

sent away into slavery, and became so hostile that the whites left.[1]

Of slaves taken in war we have very slight mention during the seventeenth century. No serious war occurred between the settlers and the natives until the Tuscarora war of 1711 and 1712. A few were captured before this and a few were imported as other slaves. So far as the laws reveal, no difference was made between them and negro slaves in regard to rights, duties, and condition of life. They were thrown closely with the negroes, and the fact that they eventually disappeared indicated that they intermarried with, and were absorbed by, the large body of blacks. Dr. Hawks is perhaps right in supposing that they were used chiefly to hunt and fish for their masters, while the harder work of the field was left to negroes.[2]

The conditions of capturing Indians for slaves are clearly shown in the account of the Tuscarora war. When the attack began Governor Hyde sent to South Carolina for aid. It is of interest to us that he directed his agent there not to fail to represent to that government "the great advantage may be made of slaves, there being many hundreds of them, women and children; may we not believe three or four thousand?"[3] History does not say what effect this argument had on the South Carolina authorities—perhaps none at all; but it does say that the Indian allies that came from the South took back a great number of slaves from the conquered people. The Indians, said Colonel Pollock, as soon as they had taken the fort and secured their slaves, marched away straight to their homes.[4] Tom Blount, chief of a tribe of friendly Indians, also had his captives for slaves. He proposed to attack a certain small tribe in which he thought

---

[1] Another reason given for their departure was the sterility of the soil. Perhaps both had something to do with it. See Lawson, History of North Carolina, pp. 73, 74; and Hawks, History of North Carolina, II., 73.

[2] Hawks, History of North Carolina, II., 229, and Brickell, Natural History of North Carolina, p. 42.

[3] Col. Recs., I., 900.   [4] Ibid., II., 30.

there might not be enough people to give each of his own warriors a slave, and he accordingly asked the Council to promise some reward, as blankets, to those who might not happen to have slaves allotted to them.[1] Most of the slaves taken in this war were sent out of the country.[2] This was probably because of the difficulty of making tractable slaves of them in their old haunts, or their liability to escape, or the friction that might arise with the unconquered remnant of the tribe if they saw their brethren continually in servitude. When the Indians took these captives they do not seem to have intended to use them any considerable time. They were taken as booty, and no doubt soon came into the possession of slave-traders. These were carried to other colonies, a good many going, it seems, to New England, since Massachusetts in 1712, and Connecticut in 1716, passed laws against the importation of Indian slaves. The objection was that they were fierce and caused trouble.[3] These slaves sold for about £10 each.[4] First and last more than 700 of them were captured and sold before the struggle was ended.

There was no further trouble with the Indians until the French and Indian wars about the middle of the century. At this time the Cherokee Indians who lived on the western frontier went to war against the English. In 1760 the Assembly raised troops to suppress the hostilities. They offered to any one who took captive " an enemye Indian " the right to hold him as a slave. If such an Indian should be killed the captor was to receive £10 from the public treasury.[5] This amount was probably less than the regular price of

---

[1] Col. Recs., II., 305.   [2] Ibid., I., 826, and II., 52.
[3] See Steiner, History of Slavery in Connecticut, Johns Hopkins University Studies, Series XI., pp. 14, 15. They seem to have kept some of the captives for themselves. For instance, the Meherrins took two children for slaves, which they possibly meant to rear as such. Col. Recs., II., 117. Women and children captured in war seem to have been saved, perhaps for slaves. Cf. Brickell, Natural History of North Carolina, 310, 311, 320.
[4] Col. Recs., II., 52.
[5] Laws of 1760 (3d session), ch. 1, sect. 13.

such slaves; for if equal to that price the captor would have been tempted to kill the captive so as to avoid the trouble of keeping him.   We have no record of how many Indians were taken in this war.   They were probably few, and were soon absorbed in the now considerable body of blacks which were being brought to the frontier.

CHAPTER V.

WHITE SERVITUDE.

The first slaves that we hear of in North Carolina were white people, and their masters were Indians. Strachey, in his *Travayle into Virginia*,[1] speaks of a story that he had from the Indians of an Indian chief, Eyanoco, who lived at Ritanoe, somewhere in the region to the south of Virginia, and who had seven whites who escaped out of the massacre at Roanoke, and these he used to beat copper. It is not improbable that there is a shadow of truth in the statement, although the details must be fictitious. That the Indians of the colony later on did enslave the whites whom they could take in their waters, or who were shipwrecked off the coast, we know from the preamble of an act of the Assembly about 1707.[2] This form of white servitude left no trace in the life of the colony.

The first laborers that the English took to the New World colonies were whites, who during the first years of their residence were obliged to serve the settlers in the capacity of bonded servants. These people were commonly called " servants " or " Christian servants," and as such are to be distinguished from slaves. In regard to them, as well as to the slaves, their history as it related to North Carolina begins in Virginia. There were three sources of the supply of these servants: 1. There were indented servants, people of no means who, being unable to pay for passage to America, agreed to assign themselves for a certain period to some ship-captain on condition that when he reached Virginia he might transfer

---

[1] Published in Hakluyt Society Publications. See p. 26.
[2] Col. Recs., I., 674.

his right for money to some one who would maintain and work the servant for the given period. 2. Transported felons, who were such criminals, vagabonds, or other obnoxious persons as were sent to the colonies by order of the English courts. 3. Kidnapped persons, usually children, who were stolen by traders or ship-captains in the London or Liverpool streets and taken to America, where they were assigned till of age to such planters as would pay the prices demanded for their passages. From these three sources many people came to Virginia during the first sixty years of its settlement. At the time, however, at which North Carolina was being settled, the importation of these people was being checked.[1] This was due to at least three causes: 1. The British government was actually exerting itself to replace the white servants with negro slaves. In this the King was interested. In 1661 the Royal African Company was organized. The Duke of York was at the head of the enterprise and the King was a large stockholder.[2] 2. The conscience of the English public was awakening to the violations of right which the traders perpetrated on those whom they allured by false promises, or forced by fraud, to go with them. These two causes acted together in 1664 when a commission of inquiry, with the Duke of York at its head, was appointed to report on the condition of such exportation of servants. At the same time arrangements were provided by which indented servants going to the colonies of their own free will might register their indentures at an office created for that purpose. Public sentiment thus aroused continued to grow until in 1686 an Order of Council was issued, which directed: (a) that all contracts between emigrant servants and their masters should be executed before two magistrates and duly registered; (b) that no adult should be taken away but by his or her own consent, and no child without the consent of the parent or master; (c) that in cases of children under fourteen

---

[1] Ballagh, White Servitude in the Colony of Virginia, Johns Hopkins Studies, Series XIII., 292-297, and 349, note.
[2] Doyle, Virginia, Maryland and the Carolinas, p. 386.

the consent of the parent as well as the master must be obtained, unless the parents were unknown.[1] The process was supplemented by an order issued in 1671 to stop the transportation of felons to the continental colonies.[2] 3. The incoming of negro slaves, who, when the experimental stage of slavery was past, were seen to be cheaper than white servants, was probably the most powerful of all the causes. The rivalry was between the whites and the blacks. The blacks won. It is impossible not to see in this an analogous process to that by which negro slavery supplanted Indian slavery in the West Indies. The abuses connected with Indian slavery touched the conscience of the people, and negroes who could better stand slavery were introduced to replace it. The abuses connected with white servitude touched the hearts of the British people, and again the negro was called in to bear the burden of the necessary labor. In each case it was a survival of the fittest. Both Indian slavery and white servitude were to go down before the black man's superior endurance, docility, and labor capacity.

The checking of the introduction of white servitude just at that time saved the colony of North Carolina for slavery. Whatever servants were now taken thither would be carried into the place in ever decreasing numbers. Another cause operated to deprive the colony of even that number of servants which would under these conditions have been its normal share. This was the poor harbors and the consequent lack of direct trade with Europe. The few ships that came through the inlets of the Currituck, Albemarle, and Pamlico Sounds brought few servants to be indented to the colonists. Furthermore, the poor economic conditions of those early days, when the farms were small[3] and the exports inconsiderable, would have made it an unsafe

---

[1] Doyle, Virginia, Maryland and the Carolinas, p. 385.
[2] Ballagh, loc. cit., 294-295.
[3] See the author's Landholding in the Colony of North Carolina, in The Law Quarterly Review (London), April, 1895, 160, 161; also cf. Col. Recs., I., 100.

venture for a trader to have tried to dispose of a shipload of servants.[1]

A few servants very probably came to the colony from the first. In the Concessions of 1665 the Proprietors offered all masters or mistresses already in the colony eighty acres of land for each able-bodied manservant whom they had brought in, armed and victualled for six months, and forty acres for each weaker servant, "as women, children, and slaves." Those who should come in during the next three years were to have sixty and thirty acres respectively instead of eighty and forty acres as just stated. Those who should come later than that should get varying other amounts.[2] This system was continued in its existing form for some time, but toward the end of the century it settled down to the habit of giving each man who came into the colony fifty acres for every person, bond or free, whom he brought in with him.[3] A further inducement was offered to the servants themselves. The Concessions of 1665 offered to every Christian servant already in the colony forty acres at the expiration of his or her period of servitude. Those coming later were to have smaller amounts. This inducement could not have brought many servants into the government, for two years later they were offered fifty acres on the expiration of their terms of service. Although this offer was not mentioned in the instructions after 1681,[4] it seems to have been allowed as late as 1737,[5] and perhaps later.

The Fundamental Constitutions, whose spirit was entirely ·

---

[1] South Carolina had good harbors, and it may be asked why it did not get more white servants. The negroes were introduced in large numbers from the first. This was due to two facts: It was somewhat later in settlement than North Carolina, and its first people came largely from Barbadoes, where slavery had been extensively in use. These men taught the colony the use of slaves from an early date in its history.

[2] The Concessions of 1665 were the first formal terms offered to prospective settlers. See Col. Recs., I., 87, 88.

[3] Ibid., I., 334; cf. also ibid., I., 865. See above, p. 17, note 2.

[4] Col. Recs., I., 334.

[5] Brickell, Natural History of North Carolina, p. 268.

feudal, provided for white servitude in that they tried to re-establish the mediæval leet men and leet women. They assumed the existence of such persons and directed that on every manor they should be subject to the lord of the manor without appeal. Such servants should not leave the lord's land without his written permission. Whenever a leet man or leet woman should marry, the lord of each should give the pair ten acres of land, for which he must not take as rent more than one-eighth of the yearly produce. It was also stipulated that "whoever shall voluntarily enter himself a leet man in the registry of the county court shall be a leet man," and "all children of leet men shall be leet men, and so to all generations." This impossible feature of an impossible system, it is needless to say, was never put into operation.[1]

In the early period of North Carolina there was continual complaint that the people harbored runaway servants. Governor Nicholson made the charge in 1691,[2] and Edward Randolph, Surveyor General, repeated the charge in 1696.[3] The situation of North Carolina was favorable to Virginia runaways, and it is likely that when servants left their masters in that province they took refuge in the swamps and forests to the southward. But there is nothing to show that North Carolina encouraged such runaways. Henderson Walker wrote in 1699 that the law for apprehending runaway negroes was adequate.[5] He must have referred to the law we find on the statute book in 1715. By that law we learn that any Christian servant who ran away from his master should on being captured be compelled to serve above his regular period of servitude double the time he was away, and in addition such longer time as the court should deem

---

[1] For a more extended discussion of the Fundamental Constitutions see the author's Constitutional Beginnings of North Carolina, Johns Hopkins University Studies, Series XII., pp. 131-139. Also see Col. Recs. on leet men, I., 191, 192.

[2] Col. Recs., I., 371, 514, 515.

[3] Ibid., I., 467.   [4] Ibid., I., 514.

sufficient to repay the master for whatever damage he may have sustained (sect. 2). This provision was incorporated in the law of 1741.[1] As many servants ran away in North Carolina itself as in Virginia, it seems. John Urmstone, who seems here to have had nothing to gain by an exaggeration, said in 1716, " White servants are seldom worth the keeping and never stay out the time indented for." [2]

The white servants fared better than the slaves. In the first place, they were vastly better than the negroes. In many instances they were people of much worth who had met with misfortune, or who having been poor in the first place had taken advantage of this opportunity to make their fortunes in the New World. Also, they were Christians and they would eventually be freemen and citizens. There was even at that time a well developed beginning of the later Southern idea which instinctively recognized the race distinction between the whites and the blacks. The law of 1715 declared that any servant over sixteen years of age who was imported without indentures should be bound out for five years, but if he were under sixteen years of age he should be bound out until he was twenty-two years of age. The age of such a servant was to be determined by the precinct court. If the master who held the unindented servant did not take him to the precinct court within six months, the period of service should be for five years. As the law of 1741 was stricter than that of 1715 in its dealings with the slave, so it was more humane in its dealings with white servants. It guaranteed the rights of the servant by providing that no imported Christian should be deemed a servant unless the importer could show a written agreement for service (sect. 1).

The rights of the master over the servant, as well as the servant's rights against his master, were fixed by law. As to the former, the law of 1715 was not very explicit; it simply provided that any servant who laid violent hands on his master or overseer should, proof being made, receive such corporal punishment as the courts should think suffi-

---

[1] Laws of 1741, ch. 24, sect. 2.   [2] Col. Recs., II., 261.

cient. The law of 1741, in this respect also milder than that of 1715, provided that disobedient servants should be tried before a justice of the peace, and on conviction by the testimony of one or more witnesses should suffer corporal punishment, not to exceed twenty lashes, as the court might determine.

On the other hand the law of 1715 required every master to provide for all his servants, imported or otherwise indented, competent diet, clothing and lodging; and it further directed that no master should " exceed the bounds of moderation in correcting them beyond their demerits." Any servant having a just complaint against his master was to go to the nearest magistrate, who should bind over the master to the next precinct court and, if he thought necessary, take a bond that the plaintiff should not be abused in the meantime. The law of 1741 reaffirmed these provisions, and added that no master should " at any time whip his servant naked without the order from a Justice of the Peace." The penalty for the violation of this law was forty shillings fine, which might be recovered by the wronged servant on petition to the county court, provided it be applied for in six months. The method of taking up such a case was as it had been in 1715, except that the case was to be tried by the county court without formal process of law, and that now the court might at discretion decide what might be the necessary diet, clothing, lodging, or correction. If the master did not agree to observe such a decision, the court was to order the said servant to be sold at public vendue for the balance of his time, the cost being deducted and the remainder of the amount realized going to the master. If, however, such a servant had become sick or in any way incapable, so that he could not be sold for enough to pay cost or charges, he should be placed in the hands of the churchwardens, and the master must provide a necessary support till the time of indenture should be expired. All servants were likewise given the right of coming into the county court without formal action in order to make complaint for their freedom, their freedom dues, or their wages.

The habit of freeing from their obligations sick or incapable servants had evidently become an abuse. The same law tried to prevent such a practice. It provided that a master discharging a sick servant before he was free and not trying to heal him should be fined £5. Such a sick servant must not be liberated if by so doing the servant " may perish or become a charge to the parish." If the law was violated in this particular the servant was sent to the churchwardens, to be supported at the charge of the master till the expiration of the period of service. But if it should appear that the servant had carelessly or viciously brought his sickness on himself, he should serve extra time, at the discretion of the court, to pay his master's loss and the cost of his recovery. This might have put the master at the mercy of his servant; but to protect him it was enacted that in this, as in all others cases of absence from service, if the servant made to the court a groundless complaint against his master he should serve after the period of indenture double the time so lost. It is impossible not to see how this may have operated to the entire injury of a friendless servant. Furthermore, it was provided that a servant put in jail should serve an extra period double the time in jail and also long enough to pay the cost of the suit. If a servant were convicted of stealing from his master he was to serve extra time, at the discretion of the court, to repay the amount of the theft. To prevent such stealing the same penalty was imposed on those who bought goods from servants that was imposed on those who traded with slaves.

The contemporary authorities usually speak in unfavorable terms of the morals of the first settlers in North Carolina.[1] It was charged that it was a place where loose living abounded. This must have been an exaggeration; yet it is possibly true that the inaccessibility of the place and the

---

[1] Brickell says: " The generality of them live after a loose and lascivious manner." Later on he adds: " There were certainly persons of both sexes temperate, frugal, good economists " (Natural History of North Carolina, p. 37).

lack of religion and education favored the incoming of a considerable undesirable element. There were, however, from the first a great many people of as good social habits as could be found anywhere. In such a condition of affairs the morals of the servants, who came closest to the more corrupt class, must have had a bad tendency. The laws of 1715 and of 1741 indicate as much. The former provided that if any woman servant bore a bastard child during her period of service she should serve two years extra, besides what punishment she should be liable to for fornication. If she came into the province with child she should not come within the provision of this act. If she were with child by her master she should be taken in hand by the churchwardens and sold for two years after the expiration of her time, the money to go to the parish. This law, it will be seen, left the offending master, whose position gave him an opportunity to be chiefly responsible for his servant's sin, entirely unpunished, except as he lost by the failure of her services or as he might be dealt with for fornication and adultery. If she were to have a child by a negro, mulatto, or Indian, she must serve her master two years extra as just stated, and over and above that she should pay to the churchwardens immediately on the expiration of that time six pounds for the use of the parish " or be sold four years for the use aforesaid."

The act of 1741 dealt with this matter more leniently. It stated that, "Whereas many women servants are begotten with child by free men or servants, to the great prejudice of their master or mistress whom they serve," accordingly, any woman servant bearing a child should for such offense be judged by the county court to serve her master for one year after the expiration of her contract. If she should be delivered of a child by her master during this period she should be sold by the churchwardens for the benefit of the church for one year after the term of service. If the father of the child were a negro, mulatto, or Indian, the mother should be sold for two years after her term of service, the money to go to the parish, and the child should be bound out by the county court till he reached the age of thirty-one years. Here again there was no punishment for the seducing master. It is also evident that the sin of the servant would be an advantage to the master, since he would thereby secure her service for a longer period. We have not the least evidence that such a thing did happen, yet it is possible that a master might for this reason have compassed the sin of his serving-woman.

These were restrictions on bastardy. As for legal union of indented servants, the Marriage Act of 1741[1] provided that no minister or civil officer should, under penalty of £5 to be paid to the master, marry any servant or servants without the written consent of the masters of the same; and that all servants so married should serve one year after the expiration of their terms. This gave the master power to prevent marriage when he should think his interests would be impaired thereby; and probably many masters used their power to prevent the marriage of servant women. At the same time it must have increased unlawful unions. It certainly seems to have been considered a hardship by the Baptists. Just before the Revolution the Kehukee Association was asked if the union of servants who had not been married according to the laws of the land should be held binding before God. The answer was " yes." Again it was asked: " Is it lawful to hold a member in fellowship who breaks the marriage of servants? " The answer was " no."[2]

The law of 1715 provided that when a master freed a Christian servant he must furnish him with three barrels of Indian corn and two new suits of wearing apparel of the value at least £5. But if the servant were a man, a gun in good condition might be substituted for one suit of clothes. These were known as freedom dues. The law of 1741 provided that, on the day of his freedom, there should be given to every servant who did not receive yearly wages, £3 proclamation money and one suit of clothes. Brickell says that

---

[1] Laws of 1741, ch. 1, sect. 7.
[2] Biggs, History of the Kehukee Baptist Association, 47 and 48.

he should also be allowed to take up fifty acres of land. He adds that most freed men preferred to sell this and become overseers for some man who had several plantations. These plantations were chiefly devoted to raising cattle, horses and hogs. An overseer was usually allowed one-seventh of the calves, foals, grain and tobacco and one-half of the pigs raised on the plantation. If he were thrifty he was soon able to stock a plantation of his own. Many thus became men of wealth and good standing. The majority, however, were not so steady. These were forced to work for their daily bread. This was the beginning of the poor whites.[1]

One other provision of the law of 1741 ought to be noticed. In the undeveloped condition of the colony it was often necessary to import skilled labor by contract. The importers of such labor often found themselves duped by the men whom they imported. It was now enacted that artisans imported under contract, who were found not to understand the trades for which they had been imported, might have their wages reduced or the contract entirely annulled on conviction in the county court. If the person who thus came in under contract should refuse to work, or absent himself from his master, he could be called into the county court and there be ordered to make satisfaction, and for every day he was idle be compelled to serve two days instead.

, In North Carolina, as elsewhere, vagrants might be made to swell the number of white servants. In 1755 the Assembly passed a law on this subject[2] which continued in force till the Revolution. It provided that all vagrants who should be taken up should " be whipped in the same manner as runaways are from constable to constable," to the counties where their wives and children formerly lived, and there give bond for good behavior, " and for betaking him or

---

[1] Brickell, Natural History, pp. 268-269.
[2] Laws of 1755, ch. 4; Laws of 1760 (4th session), ch. 13; Laws of 1766, ch. 17; and Laws of 1770, ch. 29.

herself to some lawful calling or honest labor." If they were to fail to do this they were to be hired out for one year, the money to be used in paying the expenses of the arrest, and the balance, if any, to go to the families of the said vagrants. Not only vagrants, but criminals, might be sold into servitude at the direction of the court. How much there was of this we do not know. In 1723, one Thomas Dunn, who confessed several petit larcenies, was condemned to be tied to the tail of a cart and be given thirty-nine lashes well laid on, and no one claiming him as a servant, to be sold for four years to any one who would take him out of the province.[1]

---

[1] Hawks, History of North Carolina, II., 128.

www.ingramcontent.com/pod-product-compliance
Lightning Source LLC
Chambersburg PA
CBHW020515030426
42337CB00011B/393